Shaping Your Future with 6 Dimensions of Success

DuAnne Redus

All rights reserved. No part of this book may be used or reproduced by any means, graphic, electronic, or mechanical, including photocopying, recording, taping, or by any information storage retrieval system without the written permission of the author except in the case of fair use or brief quotations embedded in critical articles or review.

Copyright © 2021 by DuAnne Redus

Cover art copyright © Artesiawells

Table of Contents

Dedication 7
   Gratitude 7

Prologue 9
   Essence Revealed 9

The Coming Home Process 14
   Resolve: Who Am I? 14
   Dissolve: Let go 14
   Involve: Go inside 14
   Evolve: Integrate 15
   Revolve: Start over/Move on 15

Dimension I: Willingness to discover, expand and evolve personal identity 16
   In the Boardroom 16
      Identities in Motion 20
      New Territory 23
      Humans look the same at one stage. 24
      Identity is Our Superpower 27
      Oral Stories 27
      Evolving Identity Archetypes to Avatars 28
      Generational Patterns 29

Dimension II: Willingness and ability to use personal voice to align with identity.............33

- Childhood Imprint.. 33
  - Head Trauma 34
  - Claim What is Yours 36
  - Ancestral Voices.. 38
  - Discerning Truth..40
  - Truth-Busting 41
  - Strengthening Voice 43
  - Power of Voice 46
  - Rio Vision.. 46
  - Power Dynamics 49
  - Voices at the Table.. 50

Dimension III: Willingness and ability to travel new paths 53

- The Yellow-Brick Road in Reverse 53
- Life Stages: Flip the Script 54
- How Did I End Up Here? 57
- Commit.. 62
- Connecting Global Spheres 62
- A Change of Plans 64
- A Teaching Intervention................................ 65
- The Castle... 66
- Warrior Spirits 69

Dimension IV: Willingness and ability to face conflict and paradox 74

    Trust or Fear 74

        Conflict in the Workplace 77

        Nothing Fails Like Success 80

        The Law of Requisite Variety 82

        Ripples in Life 84

        Organizational Paradigms 87

        Spectrum of Truth 91

Dimension V: Willingness and ability to bridge relationships in family, work, community 94

    Morphic Resonance 94

        Ancestral Wisdom 97

        A3: Acknowledge, Accept, Allow 101

        Time Collapses 105

        Fierce Love for Community 106

        A Community Story 107

Dimension VI: Ability to balance/rebalance internally as reflected by the cycles of nature 112

    Mother Nature 112

        Two Sides of the Same Coin 114

        Fusion of Science and Technology 117

        Beyond Amateur Humans 117

        The Balancing Act 119

Epilogue **120**
    The Indian Boy's Raft 120
    Summarizing Essay 122
    A Seer Sees from Behind the Eyes 122

References **134**

Dedication

Life became purposefully aligned for me when I met Sandy McDowell and Liza Charlton. Their consultancy, based in London, engaged multi-national companies in transformational development. It was an honor to be a team member on both sides of the big pond. Liza and Sandy are each an example of what it means to continually evolve and offer essential services that make the world a better place.

Gratitude

My heart has opened wider because of the supporters who believed in and encouraged me to create my legacy project. Extraordinary teachers have appeared on my continuing pathways. Tom Best led me to Don Americo Yabar in Peru. Jean Houston, renowned around the globe, appeared in my small village after decades of my learning through her mythic voice. My companions along the journey continue to walk with me sometimes holding my hand, sometimes whispering in my ear, or giving me a gentle push forward. You know who you are! Without Ashley Brown and Larry Morris with their expert skills, I might still be stuck in a perpetual loop.

Jane Vaniger who is in my writing group, recently wrote *The Balancing Act*, a poem that is spot-on to add punctuation to the final chapter. Synchronous timing!

Blueprint for Shaping Your Future

And much gratitude to Cary Graves, once a neighbor and still a sojourner, who has allowed his poem, written many years ago, to be shared.

If We Could Relearn the Way
If we could live a thousand years,
Each day wiser than the last,
We might regain an innocence,
Lost along our distant past.
We could relearn forgotten truths,
Known by the ancient sages,
About natural law, simple ways,
The wisdom of the ages.
But we must live a shorter span,
Most learning mere illusion,
Forsaking our rich innocence,
For poor man-made confusion.
When the way is lost we struggle,
With our mortal ups and downs,
As the stars smile on knowingly
At their microscopic clowns.

—Cary Graves

Prologue

Essence Revealed

Once there was a little white kitten. She was a frisky, curious cat, always exploring and discovering something new.

As she grew up and began to follow her dreams to become a tiger, she wandered farther and farther from home. As a young kitten she was very naïve, not understanding the hidden dangers in the world of cats. She developed unique ways to pounce and leap into unknown realities. She found out that her graceful body was strong. She trusted herself to adventure without a set plan.

One morning the kitten was out early in her usual manner of exploring beyond the bounds of her natural habitat. As she roamed, she smelled a scent that was new and intriguing. She found the unknown object and sniffed and poked her nose into the brightly colored bag laying on the ground. She was enticed and pushed her nose further and further into the sack until she was unable to back out. The bag encased her head. She was trapped. Her most successful backing-down-trees technique was not working.

The kitten struggled and wiggled in unusual ways, trying to get out of her stuck situation. She wandered in circles, agitated, hopelessly unable to help herself get out of something she had pushed so determinedly to get into.

Blueprint for Shaping Your Future

The kitten was exhausted when something suddenly changed: The bag came off! She found herself staring into the eyes of something she did not recognize. She was free from the constraints of her own doings. She didn't change her curious nature, but she learned to let go of expectations and not stick her head in bags again!

At an early film shoot during my corporate years, I arrived at the facility before dawn to meet the camera crew. As I sat in my car, I caught a glimpse of movement across the parking lot. *"Is it something moving in the wind?"* I wondered.

The dawning morning light revealed something alive. I got out of the car and walked towards the movement, recognizing a small white cat with its head caught in a potato chip bag! Realizing its predicament, I crept up and pulled at the bag to free the cat. Our eyes met: essence to essence, face to face.

This moment of eye contact revealed a felt sense of heart-to-heart connection. We mirrored each other without the distinction of difference, only likeness. The sense of essence was pervasive. I felt an energy of unknown origin sweep through my body. A question arose and I felt a sense of yearning. It was as if a gateway opened to follow the scent of "who am I?" I realized there was more of me that I had yet to understand.

From my studies in psychology, I was drawn to symbols. I started with archetypes that represent patterns of behavior and personality traits. The study of evolving science showed me how everything is connected energetically in systematic patterns of particles/waves, fractals, layers, and dimensions of perception. Our physical bodies are a system of organs and structures, our mental consciousness is connected to an information-collecting brain. Beyond our physical reality is a consciousness based on non-linear and energetic dimensions that include attributes we may not yet see or know about. There are unseen but sensed attributes of the energy that surrounds us, like the little white cat who reflected my essence in her eyes.

Avatars came into my awareness as symbolic imagery. Avatar literally means "descent, alight, to make one's appearance, and refers to the embodiment of the essence of a superhuman being in another form." The word implies "to overcome, to remove, to bring down, to cross something," as defined in dictionary.com. ShaMama is my avatar and resource that transcends the known and the unknown. She is both like me and opposite from me. A symbol for inner wisdom seeded from birth that represents a need to integrate the "like and unlike" me.

The entertainment industry has demonstrated the avatar concept in movies and games, making the term accessible to be understood across generations. The idea gave me another key for self-exploration that led me to the premise of this book and 6 Dimensions of identity as destiny:

    i. The willingness and ability to discover, evolve and expand personal identity.
    ii. The willingness and ability to use personal voice to align with identity.

Blueprint for Shaping Your Future

    iii.   The willingness and ability to travel new paths.
    iv.   The willingness and ability to face conflict and paradox.
    v.   The willingness and ability to bridge relationships in family, work, and community.
    vi.   The willingness and ability to balance/rebalance internally as reflected in the cycles of nature.

Quantum physics, cybernetics, natural, biological, and social science, and other areas of study have shown me sets of principles from which science operates and evolves. The wide array of knowledge presents opportunities to embrace deep and rich explorations to enhance our choices in life and work. I found it more compelling to see connections and links among many sets of information and knowledge than to compete with the seeming most real or accurate maps of reality. The frontier of human development widened for me. How we decide to interact as we develop individually and collectively is indeed energy in motion.

As an over-arching metaphor the boardroom is where decisions are made. As life unfolds in its peculiar manner the table is the central theme where every voice matters in work and life. Conference tables, kitchen tables, picnic tables or any configuration of humans who consider every voice valid that can be the funnel for positive change become petri dishes for possibility.

The collection of stories and experiences I have chosen to relate are merely a reflection of a process that continues to unfold for me personally. I am not who I once was; I am not yet who I may become; but for today, it is all I have to offer. My hope is that engaged and aspiring leaders might embrace a full pallet of magnificent personal essence as the continuing chapters of humanity are collectively scripted.

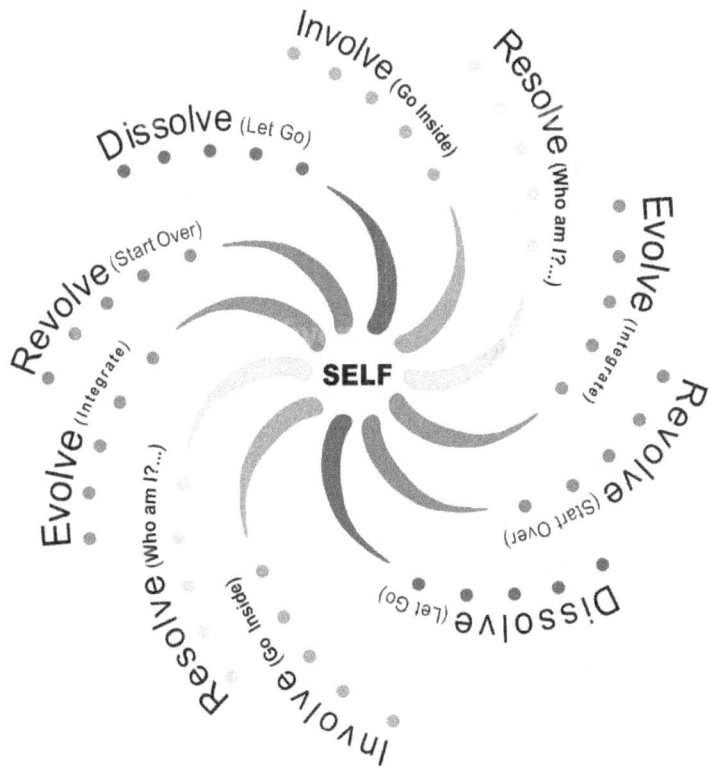

© DuAnne Redus

Blueprint for Shaping Your Future

The Coming Home Process

Resolve: Who Am I?

As we move through life questions arise from within: "Who am I? What is most important to me now? What do I really want?" These are the deep questions that begin to itch from the inside. They begin to surface from our unconscious and seep out in our dreams, or in our irritability with others. These profound questions signal that we have something to resolve about our identity. There is more to discover about our essential self.

Dissolve: Let go

The need to know "why" often gets in the way of our internal process of becoming all of who we are as a Being. We humans hold to a belief that our evolution is linear, and we hold on to prescribed ways of who we are supposed to be. When we surrender to not knowing, we enter the Mystery of life and strengthen our self-trust.

Involve: Go inside

Most of us spend much of our living experience paying attention to the outer world around us. Often, even the introverts among us are clueless about how to hear our muffled soulful voice. Taking time with our inner being allows permission for our spiritual longings to be heard through our energetic and intuitive guidance system.

Evolve: Integrate

Imagine a thousand points of light fragmented from each other. Each beam is hidden from the other beams. When integration occurs, the separate beams shape and reform to become a coherent wave of radiating visible light. Beyond words, we know we are coming home to the essence of the sacred self.

Revolve: Start over/Move on

This is the place of new beginnings. Initiatory sparks of creativity often burst forth in unexpected ways, or we see more clearly with softer eyes from the inside out. Essence connects us to something bigger than self. The matrix of life pulls us forward—again into the unknown, the uncertain and greater mystery. Something else begins to unfold.

Blueprint for Shaping Your Future

Dimension I: Willingness to discover, expand and evolve personal identity

If you're not at the table, you're probably on the menu.

—Elizabeth Warren,
U.S. Senator

—Ann Richards,
Former Texas Governor

In the Boardroom

Sitting in an oversized comfortable leather chair too tall for my feet to touch the floor, I adjust the chair height and roll up to the conference table. The meeting room has a panoramic eastern view of the Oquirre mountains as I gaze towards the windows from the 13th floor meeting room with an inviting outside balcony. Seven others enter the room and find a seat.

The only female on the executive team of a technical engineering company, I take in stride the fact that I am fortunate to be a team member. Irrelevant chatter among us eventually subsides as we get down to business. We begin our weekly executive meeting as the high-ranking professional gives his update.

He begins with bravado about his accomplishments. I begin to realize he has broken the commitments agreed to by our team the week before. In fact, he reports a totally different set of actions than our agreed strategy. Breaking an agreement is not something I take lightly.

My body heats up - literally. The heat rises from the bottom of my feet, up my calves, into my solar plexus, up my throat. My head feels like it's about to explode. My vocal cords feel slightly constricted as I begin to probe. "Was there a specific reason you changed our strategy? Did something change? Was anyone else on the team consulted?" No one else spoke up. I brought the obvious contradiction to the table as every other person pushed chairs backwards as if distancing themselves from the truth of the situation.

My mind could not grasp that it was acceptable to the others in the room pretend we were all on the same page. But the unwritten code of conduct in the leader-dominant culture of the organization required us not to challenge or confront him. In lieu of reporting directly to the executive, we would wait until after the meeting to complain among ourselves lacking the courage to face the truth. Although I was a valued member of the team, I believed I did not have the clout to make waves for fear of being labeled "whiny." As a single mother, I needed this job to complete my academic education which the company was funding as part of my compensation package.

This time was different, though. My body signaled loudly that something needed to change. At least needed to change for me. This time I decided to listen to my physical cues. My team members often confessed they were uncomfortable confronting the boss in a group setting. They preferred to "work behind the scenes" to lobby for alternative negotiated outcomes which led to distrust. For me, it was time to see, hear and feel my personal reality. I was ready to acknowledge I was uncomfortable because breaking agreements was out of alignment with my values. I decided I wanted to sit at a table that allowed open, transparent communication and decision making that would give me the opportunity to create the menu. My exit strategy began to form.

Other professionals, male and female, have shared similar experiences about feeling unseen, unheard, and disregarded as valued humans in their workplaces. The impetus for using my voice for positive change was born in that heated experience.

What I came to understand through my continuing professional and personal development is that identity creates destiny. Who we think we are sets up the framework of our beliefs, values, and behaviors. The ageless question, "who am I?" is the basis for how we create our lives. Yet, it is one of those questions that gets bypassed in the busyness of working to meet quarterly short-term goals and/or put food on the family table.

It also occurred to me that the companies and organizations where people work also have obscure identities shrouded by branding and marketing strategies often disconnected from the humans who produce, design, and create goods and services.

DuAnne Redus

My career blossomed and crisscrossed between psychology, business and organizational behavior. My quest became exploring the what, the why and the how work gets accomplished, satisfies, sustains, aligns, or misaligns with long-term health and well-being of the entities where work happens.

To the readers, whether you are already an engaged leader or an aspiring purposeful leader, I offer a hint that this book is not a sequential delineation about how to discover and expand your identity, although I hope that you may see the mirror of your unfolding self within the stories of people and organizations presented. If you have an inkling or a strong desire that work and life can be sustaining and aligned with the gift of who you are beyond an amateur human, jump into the unraveling mystery. There are infinite paths to discover according to our willingness and intent to be our most extraordinary self.

© Kittipong Jirasukhanont

Blueprint for Shaping Your Future

Identities in Motion

> *Every being, every organization is an identity in motion, creating itself in the world and creating its world simultaneously.*
>
> —Margaret J. Wheatley, Ph.D.,
> *Leadership and the New Science*

We are midwives of our own birthings. An identity in motion describes how my personal experience has unfolded beyond the many roles I have played in life and work. Examining how time has unfurled in my life, I divide segments of time into trimesters like I experienced as a mother carrying a child. First there was a seed, then birthing and development, and letting go when the child was ready to fly.

I see birth through 30 years as a beginning that is unscripted. Then come the surprise wake ups and try-outs to become an adult. The third trimester holds the possibility of living beyond ego, inside the scope of wisdom and mystery, willing to navigate without a cheat sheet of answers about how it is supposed to be. The number of age doesn't really matter, because I've come to realize that life can continue to evolve indefinitely, beyond what we have been conditioned to understand.

As a baby boomer I was an outlier to the hippie culture that bloomed in the 1960s. Nor did I understand the culture that stood up for civil rights or those sent to fight in Viet Nam. My sense of self was limited to fit into the small world of a conservative environment in the Texas panhandle under the wings of generations who had fought war after war for their right to be free. The paradigm of war is traumatizing and painful. The generations before me wanted to forget and move beyond painful memories. For the most part they were without strategies to heal from atrocities of war. Most held on for the ride hoping for a better future for the next generation.

What stands out to me in my childhood memories is the nurturing, caring and comfort I viscerally felt from my maternal and paternal grandparents. A form of essence was revealed to me for which I had no words or mental understanding. I connected to a felt sense of something true and lovable about myself. Living on the high plateau where the sky met the flat barren ground gave me a sense of space. Wide open horizons became a living concept that I wanted to feel inside my body. I longed to feel free.

New concepts were intriguing to me. I remember studying Egyptian cosmology in grade school which led me to study goddess archetypes. Maybe it was my ego, but I was magnetized and eventually claimed the attributes of goddess as a template to recognize grace and beauty in myself. Throughout my life passages I have been attracted to other archetypes. As an initiator of ideas, I looked for creative outlets that took me down various trails into my self-discovery. Jumping forward in time, I can see how my ShaMama avatar became a metaphor to integrate positive and negative experiences beyond conflict and towards creative ideas. Explicating and aligning my values and beliefs brought me to a center beyond my biases. A peaceful center like the calm in the eye of a tornado. The winds could be blowing around me, and yet I could find a still point from which I was able to watch as an observer.

My ShaMama avatar is an embodied sense of essence that encapsulates positive feelings and sense of knowing beyond what my mind can grasp or explain. Her presence is like "mothering-fathering" wisdom. Internal stirrings, familiar to my feminine nature, are complemented by my initiating, risk-taking proclivities that balance and counterbalance my personality with the grace of essence. A warrior goddess, ShaMama embodies how to stand in the fierceness of love as a wisdom seeker and soul whisperer. She sees from the inside beyond my human eyes. She began to reveal herself to me in my second trimester during my 40s, first coming to me in my sleeping dreams and in occasional spontaneous moments as my sense of self was expanding into a voice I hesitantly began to accept as mine.

Circumstances of our lives often invite us to deep-dive into the uncertainty we face daily. There were times I accepted the invitation. Most of the time I declined. Before I turned thirty, my mantra was "keep safe. Hold on. Don't rock the boat." I sought to stay safe and out of the way of others who seemed confident about who they were and what they wanted while I had no idea who I was or wanted to be. I meandered.

DuAnne Redus

New Territory

Eventually, my career presented me with the opportunity and gift to work internationally with CEOs and other C-suite executives and their teams to birth individual and corporate identities. Our work together was not about branding! We were midwives who supported the unfolding development of people in the work settings with methodologies that allowed them to become creators and shapers of a cultural environment that nourished the workers. Evaluating projects through the rearview mirror, the most common feedback from participants had a theme: "Why didn't I find out sooner who I really am?" Often it was at the peak of a career that the idea of personal essence could be woven into the domain of work.

As amateur humans most of us have given up the possibility that life and work can be synchronized. Historically the earliest forms of life were integrative, simple and straightforward: Hunt. Gather. Sleep and awaken with the sun. But as the complexity of life has exponentially increased, I wonder why humanity has not progressed and adapted in ways that move towards collective well-being? We are living in an era that is literally showing us how we can move towards becoming more enlightened in our choices. Chasms, fractures, and disruptions are occurring on a global scale. What might it mean if our work complemented our beingness in the world?

Metamorphosis means transforming or changing shape. What does it mean to be fully developed? Is it when we metamorphosize from immature to adult form

Blueprint for Shaping Your Future

in two stages like an insect or amphibian? Or when we change the nature of a human into a different one like a robot? Technically, we humans are Homo Sapiens, from the Latin meaning 'one who knows'. Knows what? ShaMama has been whispering to me, *Sapien Sapiens*. One who knows the one who knows? It's something of a thought puzzle. One of my favorite poets is Rumi, the 12th century Persian poet whose voice flows with metaphors about identity.

Creation unfolds like calm breakers. Constant, slow movement teaches us to keep working like a small creek that doesn't stagnate but finds a way through numerous details deliberately.

Deliberation born of joy like a bird from an egg. Birds don't resemble eggs! Think how differently the hatching out is. A white leathery snake egg, a sparrow's egg, a quince seed, an apple seed; very different things look similar at one stage.

These leaves, our bodily personalities, seem identical, but the globe of soul fruit we make, each is deliberately unique.

—Rumi

Humans look the same at one stage.

In Rumi's way of thinking, essence is not synonymous with 'special'. Essence is not hierarchical, ranking or comparing one above another. Essence is like air. Air can be described in various forms: cold air, hot air and steaming air, each with distinctions. Essence relates to character and can morph if we increase our inner frequency to higher vibrations of lightness and joy.

I learned in Peru from indigenous people in the high Andes that one's energy can be heavy or light. Their deeply spiritual souls are tuned in to nature in ways that are easy to perceive. They showed me that heavy energy is dark and supported by negativity and fear. I learned how to lighten my energy with concentration and focus and letting go of fearful thoughts and emotions when I accepted that I am literally responsible for my energy patterns. Cleaning our energy is a real thing! Not only did I discover more about myself, but others in my life also began to see me differently.

In the human endeavor there is opportunity for each of us to discover personal truths, truths others hold, and higher, universal truths, if we are open and attentive without judgment. Getting to truths of essence is a lifelong process that flows like a river. What seed are you birthing? Or might be lying dormant?

An acorn falls to the ground in its own time. Maybe it will decay and feed the earth. Maybe it will become food for somebody. Maybe it will be nurtured and become a mighty oak. As amateur humans we typically put little focus on who we are and the importance of our personal development. The more I nurture my inner sensibility, the more options become apparent.

Our usual path is to bump our way around obstacles with little focus and few perceived choices.

Blueprint for Shaping Your Future

Some of us attempt to mold ourselves to replicate someone else's beliefs. Many of us decide on a plan and commit to the suffering or motivation required to prove it can be accomplished. Even more of us attempt to break away from the plan someone else imagined for us. The ideas in this book are intended to add choices in life that are rich and fertile. Perhaps, these choices are not yet seen or understood.

In the present complex environments on the planet, I find it useful to look through many lenses using the 6 Dimensions of insight that center on who we are as human beings. Sensing and noticing patterns, these inner dimensions are variations of what we as humans believe to be reality. Some talk of parallel dimensions. Others talk about multiverses. For me, the dimensions weave together in an ongoing process.

The metaphor of refracted light through a prism can be applied to humans if we consider our energetic and emotional realms. In the first trimester of our lives, we have an embedded multi-dimensional compass. The ability to interpret the compass can be nourished or truncated in conditioned environments. If a child is raised in a fearful, unsafe, or unhealthy environment the compass is interpreted differently than if the environment is safe and the conditions are healthy. The compass doesn't change, but the ability to interpret does.

Referring to the 6 Dimensions listed in the prologue, it can be useful to reframe the Dimensions as inquiries into the self.

Identity is Our Superpower

Sometimes asking a question is a way to get a sneak peek. Using premises of the 6 Dimensions can be informative to explore:

1. How do I identify who I am in this moment? Perhaps there is an archetype that resonates with me.
2. Am I expressing my voice? Is a message forming or clear?
3. Am I willing to explore other, perhaps unfamiliar paths?
4. Am I acknowledging and facing conflict or paradox in my life or work?
5. Is there a bridge or intersection to cross or explore with family members, a relationship, co-worker, or community leader?
6. Where and how am I out of balance? Am I stuck in the tick-tock world? Have I noticed the cycles of nature around me?

Oral Stories

One of the stories told to me by the elders of the Andes seems relevant in our evolving collective timeline. A long time ago, Creator came to Turtle Island, divided the people into four directions and said, "You must go through the cycles of time separately, but one day you will come back together to share the learnings you have experienced while you were apart." Creator sent people to live in each of the four directions,

Blueprint for Shaping Your Future

holding them accountable to share their unique learning experiences for the earth and each other.

Evolving Identity Archetypes for Avatars

When my grandchildren were playing games and collecting Pokémon cards in the 1980s, I was struck with the sense they were learning the language of energy, i.e., earth/air/fire/water. They were able to see the representations of the Japanese figures in ways that reflected information most adults didn't recognize as relevant to life. Energetic forces were apparent to the children without complicated explanations.

As technology has evolved, the gaming industry has escalated the idea of avatars into advanced thinking and imagination. Simulations offer experiences once limited to NASA. We use emojis to represent our image and emotions in social communications. The movie industry has parlayed avatars into human reflections that can be easily recognized. Artificial intelligence can take us into experiences in which we seemingly have no control. We hear people referring to their superpowers as if we can generate a new supply at will! The metaphor intrigued me as I began to think more deeply about archetypes relevant to me.

My attention and magnetic interest in archetypes blew open through the years. Again, the insight has influenced the continuous unveiling of who I am in parallel with who I am becoming. It's a continuous process. When I watched the film, *The Last Avatar*, Kalki was depicted as the Avatar of Truth. Beautifully scripted and illustrated, the film demonstrated the stirring to bring forth wisdom in the *re-membering* of our core being, the seed incubated at birth.

ShaMama sees the possibility that engaged and aspiring leaders might well be writing to me, the Elder, because wisdom seems to be much closer to the surface in many of the those born in recent decades. For my generation of Baby Boomers born in 1946 to 1964, layers of remembered historical trauma covered up wisdom long buried. As historical facts are revealing what has been hidden from view, youth have access to information that allows a re-evaluation of how they envision the future. The guidance of elders as deep listeners is a gift that once existed. Where are the elders?

Generational Patterns

I freed a thousand slaves. I could have freed a thousand more if only they knew they were slaves.
—Harriet Tubman

Repeated behaviors are coded and imprinted in our biology. The patterns in generational timelines of repeated wars and domination became obvious through lives of the Silent Generation of the late 1930s and 1940s. Silent, unspoken stories embedded with trauma and no outlet to reconcile the atrocities of war or to speak about untold heroism. Wanting to forget, not feel or remember, they put their hopes into boomers who became noted as the 'me' generation. We took up the mantle of a more prosperous future that has manifested into a burgeoning consumptive standard of life. Yes, boomers are not all the same ilk, although social science has been able to quantify major patterns.

On the other side of the coin, as a boomer I see the need to bridge the fractures and chasms that separate us into a similar cohort group. Many stories are untold or unheard among us. My desire is to open new conversations. Support and nurturance will bolster those who are willing and equipped to lead positive global change that can re-script rather than continue a misguided and outdated script. If identity is destiny, we are shifting towards becoming mature, integrated identities that care for both the individual and the collective. New archetypes are showing up as Community Weavers, Visionary Explorers, Creative Architects, Earth Healers and more. I learned to see patterns within organizations. I began to see examples of this kind of symbolism with my clients.

The Chief Executive Officer of an organization (CEO) has a personal identity that is often not recognized by direct-report team members. Typically, it is easy to see imprints of an organization's identity because of marketing strategies externally visible in logos and other marketing collateral materials. My experiences with CEOs revealed misalignments between executives and their teams. One executive described to me that he imagined his team on a large, well-equipped ship heading toward a desired destination. When I inquired how and where he saw himself in relation to his team members, he remarked he experienced himself on the shoreline, not on the ship. It then became apparent that his team felt as if there was no Captain. As we worked together, the CEO took responsibility to claim part of his identity as a Visionary taking a long view of where the ship was heading as he stood on the deck. He also realized he needed to surround himself with translators of his vision into a story that included his staff and the entire organization which required some reorganizing into a less hierarchical reporting structure.

 An Executive Vice President (EVP) of a world-wide technical team brought me into her organization because of communication issues among her diverse staff. Her reports had multi-cultural backgrounds including Persian, German, and Hispanic, adding multiple layers of nuance to communication patterns and the expectations of their leader. She was determined to remedy the disconnects among her team to ensure collective success.

 Because it was distracting to meet with the team in their busy work environment, I invited each team member to come to the beach for our one-to-one coaching sessions. Sitting under umbrellas in comfortable beach chairs allowed each person to relax and reflect in a pleasing environment.

 During my time with the EVP, we often walked on the beach. She told me that she saw herself as an Australian sheep dog whose nature was to herd the animals in a safe direction. She agreed that her model as a leader was not giving her the team the results she

Blueprint for Shaping Your Future

wanted or had expected. When I asked her how she saw herself at home and in other domains of her life, she shifted her demeanor. Smiling, she replied, "Oh, I am an exotic cat who is relaxed, laid back and curious." When she updated her belief that she could lead from her true essence, she was able to change her behaviors. Instead of herding her team, she began to allow each person to bring their differences into the model of communication to clarify, understand and perform their objectives. The dynamics of her team changed for the better.

Who we think we are underlies our thoughts and ways of Being. While our roles may be different in work life and home life, it is important for us as developing humans to bring forth the essence of our uniqueness. Sometimes an archetype or avatar can highlight those essential qualities demonstrating a clear and unique sense of self.

DuAnne Redus

Dimension II: Willingness and ability to use personal voice to align with identity

It took me quite a long time to develop a voice, and now that I have it, I am not going to be silent.
—Madeleine K. Albright

Yesterday I was clever, so I wanted to change the world. Today I am wise, so I am changing myself.
—Rumi

Childhood Imprint

An early memory as a child of 4 or 5 years of age is an example of not having a voice 'at the table.' We were a family of four. We had one car. Mother had given up her teaching for a time. Daddy worked eight to five, five days a week. On this day, Mother had the car for errands. We picked Daddy up from the office at 5 pm. "How was your day, darling?" Mother inquired of Daddy. He shrugged as he replied with slumped shoulders, "It was a difficult day. I fired Joe".

My sister and I were in the backseat. When I heard the words, 'fired Joe', my mind immediately created an image of Daddy lighting a fire under Joe, probably resembling the cowboy and Indian movie scenes of early television. My young undeveloped brain gave me no way to interpret his words other than literally. One of our family rules was 'do not interrupt the adults' even if we had a question. Trapped in my mind without an escape hole. What an imprint!

I was a budding teener before I began to logically sort out literal from imaginative because I hung out in a dreamy, ungrounded space most of the time. Daydreaming is real. It took me out of my body. Those made-up myths taught to children about Santa and the Easter Bunny became fuzzy confusion in my brain as I tried to please everyone in my surroundings by playing the game of believing what I was told. I did not yet know how to reconcile daydreams and myths with the reality of life. I did not know how or where in my body to notice or perceive nuances: my heart, my head, or my gut?

I noticed something inside me; I couldn't tell where in my body. I didn't know how to discern my sensory experiences. I became a Seeker on a mission to question life more deeply.

Head Trauma

An early experience of diving into a swimming pool that was too shallow to be safe presented me with a knot on my noggin and a fear of diving. Snippets of memories shape our emotions and can come back as a surprise later in life. I found out that fear laid hidden until adulthood.

As a maturing young adult, I joined a women's group for self-empowerment. It was early summer, an outdoors adventure day. We were working to find inner strength experientially in the rugged outdoors. One of the tasks was to climb a 40-foot pole that had pegs for foot support to assist in the climb. At the top of the pole was a 15" circular disc mounted horizontally. Fitted with climbing harness, safety ropes and helmet, we were asked to climb to the top, stand on the disc and leap into the abyss as an act of trust.

    It was easy to begin the climb, but my arms began to tire. Team members on the ground hollered with positive reinforcement. Finally, I reached the top and managed to stand on the disc. I froze, paralyzed. My body felt balanced. I wanted to stay where I was, safe on two feet. My mind told me I was insane to take this physical risk. I have no memory of how long it was before embarrassment swept through me. "Are you a chicken? Take a chance!" I heard from the women looking up at me. At last, I held my nose with two fingers as if I was jumping into a pool of water. I leapt into my deepest fear, not even aware that my fear had been seeded by my childhood dive into the shallow end of a swimming pool.

    On the ground as the safety ropes were released, I surrendered. My voice manifested in traumatic cries. Weeping, I lay on the earth, realizing I had been incapsulated in a literal mind trap that prevented me from trusting myself. The childhood memory that 'headfirst' was not safe had entrapped me. This was a beginning step for me to return to my body from which I had most often been disconnected for thirty-plus years, somehow fearful that it was not a safe place. The inward process of self-trust began as I entered my second trimester and began to synchronize to my inner voice.

More self-development programs followed. I was hungry to know more about me. By now I had a good job in the corporate world that reimbursed employees for continuing education. I enrolled in courses that spanned months. At the end of an eighteen-month study, I declared to a group that I was ready to claim my personal power. The words came out of my mouth as an act of courage, but my voice quivered. A deeper sense of myself pervaded my cells. My new voice was starting to come out. Words matter. Where and when does my voice matter?

This was significant because it was from that point that I began to have dreams that informed me from my other-than-conscious knowing. One dream became part of my living reality reflected in my evolving identity.

Claim What is Yours

I dreamed I had gone to visit a friend in another country. When I arrived, my friend was out, so her adult son invited me to go for a walk until she returned.

We went outside into a beautifully wooded area with a worn and winding footpath like a deer trail. Shortly on our path, someone stepped in front of me from the left, and handed me a small stick about six inches in length. When I accepted the stick, it turned into a small lizard! We walked a little further when someone came from my right and handed me a stick about twelve inches in length. In my hand this longer object transformed into a garden snake, harmless and wiggly. I shrugged my shoulders with a question mark on my face, not understanding what was happening. We walked farther and a third person came towards me with a tall, staff like walking stick. When it was offered to me, I pulled back thinking to myself, "I know this game, and I am not playing." An inner voice of authority spoke to me, "Take what is yours, NOW!" Intuitively, I knew this was a choice point. Hesitantly I reached out and accepted the tall staff which instantly turned into a cobra. Green eyes stared me in the face. I stopped cold, stunned, afraid. Looking at the viper I asked, "Are you going to kill me?" The reply was "No, you have claimed what is yours."

The dream affirmed what my mind was only beginning to accept: I was entering a transition in my life - initiation. Later when I was rereading my dream journal, the symbols were apparent. The small stick represented a pencil or stylus for writing my truths. The middle-sized stick represented a 'talking stick" used in Native American cultures to hold when speaking in a circle signifying speaking my truths. The tall stick symbolized accepting the staff of life, to walk my truth. Tangible and intangible realities merged.

There are numerous ways to analyze dreams. My experience continues to be that dreams bridge between the visible and invisible realities that merge into present time. My sleep dreams translate intuition into images, symbols, shapes, and sounds that allow me to discern inner wisdom that I can bring forward in my living experience. Thirty-plus years of dream journals reveal

Blueprint for Shaping Your Future

significant twists and turns of my personal journey that mesh with my 'real' tangible life.

Some believe personal development occurs naturally with no need to explore. My belief is that a foundation of exploration is prerequisite to uncover and express unconceived possibilities. Once we find our inner voice, it is important to express that voice. What do I have to say that aligns with who I am? Just because we get a place at the table does not mean we have a voice at the table. I was awakened to recognize that I have messages to share which may or may not be accepted.

Ancestral Voices

Long, long ago, personal development occurred in community under supervision by Elders who provided initiations and ceremonies to signify change and growth. The concept of naming a new being was considered as a seed for character and potential. Voices of the tribe or clan as a community, nourished and supported life journeys. Tribes and clans were socially constructed to nurture every person. For example, the role of the grandmother listened to the voices within her group and advised the warriors. Her intuitive guidance was offered to the scouts who watched for external dangers. Listening for internal guidance may come through to us in modern times as imprints from our ancestors if we choose to tune in.

DuAnne Redus

© Emelena2015

Do you claim your voice or is it preempted by a sense that it has been stolen? Gaps in our current humanity present us with dilemmas. Human or humanoid? Amateur humans or fully human? We are all born, but the process of becoming truly *sapien sapiens* only begins at moments of nakedness as we move into unknown realities. Peering into the eyes of a newborn when they awaken into body form does not reveal an empty vessel. One can intuit something more

Blueprint for Shaping Your Future

by looking deeply into opening eyes. Our first voice comes from the place of dependency, crying out or laughing.

Discerning Truth

Identity theft is rampant. Who does the programming of our brains as we grow? Are we artificial victims or unaware humans? Humans are organic beings with memories, visions, and dreams. Robotic tools allow surgeons to operate on the tiniest of hearts using knowledge and skill. Humanoids are robots with human-like appearances that allow interaction with tools or environments made for humans. Additionally, there are now cyborgs that combine an organism with a machine such as an artificial limb. Artificial intelligence is indeed artificial, according to algorithms concocted by humans. Programmed commands preempt the 'knowing' voice.

Information and knowledge are useful but not as powerful as once believed because of instant accessibility. Einstein once said that 'knowledge is only a blunt instrument without the spirit behind it."

The following story reveals what I discovered about myself in my early adulthood.

DuAnne Redus

Truth-Busting

It was unusually hot for a May day in tornado alley. I walked slowly from the student parking lot across campus to my last final exam. "My first college semester at Midwestern University is almost history," I mused. Sweaty and getting drippier by the step, my body felt heavy, dreading the speech that would be the format of our exam.

The second-story classroom was still and muggy even though the wood-framed, wide windows were raised on three sides of the high-ceiling room. *So much for looking cool and collected.* With seventeen of us at three minutes each, I calculated to figure out how long we might be held hostage to earn our way out of the class with 75% of our final grade resting on this the most dreaded speech. How could I be prepared for a surprise topic?

And now the waiting game. When would the professor call my name? "Miss Redus, are you with us?" Everyone was staring at me. Up and to the front of the room I went. I hurried with a thousand sound bites in my head. "Keep your arms down so the wet spots won't show. Stand straight, look confident and smile; don't talk too fast; make eye contact around the room." I reached into the fishbowl to draw a topic for the impromptu talk.

Moonshine in the Cellar.

What a curious subject. Well, go for it. "It was a hot summer night in the two-story colonial mansion." I began to paint a vivid picture of a young, enamored

Blueprint for Shaping Your Future

couple sneaking into the dark, cool cellar to find a private place. I described a full moon shining through the high windows filling the room with a mellow kind of ambiance. Snickers filtered into my ears as I noticed lots of smiles on the mostly male faces around the room. "Keep going, you're getting warmed up," I thought with my fuzzy logic. I amped up the romantic vibe with an impassioned deep kiss when I saw the timekeeper flag the 30-second signal.

Guffaws of laughter and clapping thundered into my ears. I walked to the professor to pick up my grade, A+. He looked me directly in the eyes. "You really don't know what moonshine is, do you?" Blushing, I returned to my seat with a 'there's more to this story' feeling in my body. I created a new belief in that moment that it was not a bad thing to not know what I didn't know. For many, not-knowing is uncomfortable. I know that *not knowing* gave me the gift of accepting my voice in my own experience. A new definition was formed in my mind that truth can be discerned and updated. I learned to truth-bust.

Truth-busting is an approach to call out so-called truths that we have been conditioned to believe. A method to delve into self-development to bridge incomplete stories, e.g., between generations. Truth-busing is a strategy I have employed for personal development that continues to be useful.

It has often been said that when we are ready a teacher/mentor/guide appears, often disguised or unrecognizable to our rational brain! ShaMama is my unified example as I have continued to speak the voice she represents: an inner guide that waits to be embodied as a messenger.

Strengthening Voice

On the way to the first executive meeting with our client in Leeds, England, I noticed a billboard on the turnpike. Beneath the large image of a red sports car were the words 'Designed for Power-Hungry Americans'. *What a curious advertisement*, I mused. I laughed because there was a double-edged resonance of truth. America has a reputation as rugged individuals. Many fled England to declare independence! The other side of the truth stung. I had an immediate sense of how readily people hold each other hostage with judgments disguised in sarcasm.

When we arrived at the conference, I announced in my introduction to the eight male executives, "I am the power-hungry American depicted on your billboard with the red sports car." I requested that they might withhold final judgment about me till the end of our project. This icebreaker turned out to be useful as I met with 15 groups of 25 people over the next months. Bit by bit we took time to peel away the layers of thought that could have stymied our learning together. We examined personal and corporate beliefs that appear from the depths as resistance to change. Literally, I was clueless that my relationship to language was about to turn itself upside down and inside out.

One group of managers became the key to my expanded understanding of how words can limit our

Blueprint for Shaping Your Future

actions. It was the evening before our final session. The small manor turned into a country hotel was a refuge where I stayed often in Yorkshire. Each night after dinner, I went for a walk along a narrow pathway lined by ancient tree beings who stood like sentinels between time. Often, I marveled at how familiar they seemed. When I lingered to rest my body close to a chosen one, I felt a connection that reminded me I was not alone on my extended travels from home.

During my walk that crisp final evening, I pondered the conclusion of my relationship with this first group, wishing I had a gift for each person. The shallow stream behind the hotel beckoned me. I walked slowly, unfocused and decided to choose a rock for each participant as my parting gift. My next step stumbled on the first rock. I leaned over to claim its beauty. When I picked it up for inspection, I realized it was more like a piece of concrete from a garden curb than a real rock. It was so ordinary I didn't want it.

As I flung my arm outward to throw it aside, an inner voice spoke to me. "Who are you to name me not a rock?" Astounded, I stopped and took another look at the piece of stone-like material I held in my gloved hand. "Who gets to name me a rock?" the voice asked again. "What if I am an emerging rock, coming into my own? And in my own time?" Now I was intensely confounded. Slowly I began a process of truth-busting that led me to understand how easy it is to judge something or someone with simple language. Naming what is so or not so, according to subjective opinions. Carefully, reverently, I placed the *rock* in my coat pocket. Back in my small cozy room with the groaning steam heat, I carefully washed each stone I had collected and felt gratitude for my new awareness.

    The next morning when we opened our final session, I carried a tray around the room with the stones meticulously arranged, asking each person to choose their handpicked gift from nature. After each stone had been chosen, I asked who had taken the rock shaped like a rectangular cube. The director who had selected it spoke up. I told the story of how easily I had sat in judgment unaware of how I had limited possibility. "Patrick, you are holding the rock almost named not a rock." Everyone laughed, perhaps not fully grasping the profound depth of my experience.

© Ivan Sazykin

Blueprint for Shaping Your Future

My final assignment to the participants was to value their rock, give it importance and pass it on to someone in the future as a unique symbol. I suggested they decide who would receive the gift with the intent that the recipient would be honored to receive it. Patrick, holding the now infamous rock, held it up and exclaimed, "I am not giving away this rock. I have named it Good Fortune!" There is no telling what stories that little rock might share with us now. It had become a jewel to one who understood.

Power of Voice

Another project with a group of engineers gave me more insight into the power of voice. We were in a large ballroom at a resort where the participants had each hung a poster of their hand-drawn vision for the future of the company.

At the end of their individual sharing, one engineer asked me a question: "And what is your next vision?" I was taken aback, and before I had time to think about the answer, I heard myself say out loud to the group, "I want to work internationally in different cultures." Boom! Within six months, I was part of an international team.

Rio Vision

My dream of working with an international team came true when, a few years later the principals of the consultancy invited us to join them in Rio de Janeiro to celebrate a significant birthday during Carnival.

Happily, I accepted. An experience that literally carried me into my next vision was unexpected and powerful.

New experiences as a group of open-minded consultants were embedded in our continuous learning. The gauntlet was laid. *Find a way to challenge yourself during our time together!* Our hotel was on the Copacabana Beach where I could see hand gliders zooming out over the ocean. My curiosity led me to inquire how I could take a flight.

After interviewing several pilots, I scheduled an early flight. Several of my colleagues volunteered to be witnesses. The launch site was on Sugarloaf Mountain, a peak on a peninsula that juts out into the Atlantic Ocean. The pilot, Rogerio, picked us up in a jeep loaded with gliders. We arrived at the launch site, which was totally covered in low-hanging clouds with no visibility to the ocean.

Nevertheless, Rogerio hooked us up for the tandem flight. We were first in line, but he told me that we would only fly if he saw a break in the clouds. "If I see a way, I will look at you and ask, 'are you ready?'. If you say no, we will step aside to clear the way for the next craft. If you say yes, I want you to run as hard as you can toward the clouds."

It was an easy choice for me. I was at a precarious point in my life, and ready for a new vision having lost my husband a few months earlier. When Rogerio popped the question, I yelled, 'yes' and ran to the edge. Within seconds we broke through the cloud cover and began circling over the beach and ocean. Having the

Blueprint for Shaping Your Future

perspective of an Eagle, I felt a new vison shaping within my body. Intuitively I knew and felt a sense of confidence that my life would continue to unfold in ways I could navigate, even amid ambiguity and uncertainty. My challenge was overcome, and for this I am continually grateful.

Have you been in situations or in groups meant to discuss ideas or strategies to solve a problem, create a new product or service, or make decisions that affected others? Of course, you have! Were there times when you shared an idea and not one person responded? Was it as if no one heard you, thereby disregarding or negating the idea? As a result, did you shut down, speak louder, or more energetically attempt to sell the idea?

Did someone else suggest the same idea as the discussion continued? Did others accept and praise the idea as if it had not previously been offered? Did you sit in stunned silence, nod, or smile while you felt invisible or betrayed? Voiceless?

The patterns that mold our behaviors happen early in life. What role did you play in your family of origin? Were you the Pleaser, trying to keep everyone happy? The Peacekeeper, the Referee, the Mediator, Clown, Pathfinder or Scout? Learned family dynamics, if not recognized and clarified in adulthood, are carried over into work environments. The behavioral patterns I studied in psychology and in my personal family experience began to show themselves in workplaces. The overt and covert power structures popped into my understanding and awareness.

Power Dynamics

As I became a change agent inside organizations our team began to assess the functioning of client projects on a scale of healthy or unhealthy. Was there a high degree of increasing structural and functional complexity or decline? We observed interactions. Which members were given permission to speak freely or with hesitation? Were all members given the opportunity to participate? Who directed the exchanges among team members? Communication patterns were highly valuable to discern effectiveness of leadership styles relating to power dynamics in leadership roles.

At the lower end of power relationships was evidence of chaos and low levels of effective leadership relating to task performance. Sometimes the pattern presented as a three-ring circus exhibiting lack of clarity or confused boundaries. Often a chaotic structure was rigid and stereotyped, allowing for little flexibility and a repeating cycle of frustration for employees.

Dominance by one leader is a pattern of behavior that attempts to use control and creates dominant-submissive relationships. This highly structured and authoritarian leadership style shows up with interpersonal boundaries that are rigidly held. The message is 'stay in your lane.' Silos of expertise may be contained, prohibiting honest communication. The engineering team may be isolated from the sales team as an example. Sales or service viewpoints gained from their clients might not be sufficiently explained to the engineers designing the criteria for product development, thus creating a gap.

Blueprint for Shaping Your Future

Organizational systems with high adaptability and flexibility allow for more lateral exchange and development of relationships and creativity. Shared leadership begins by allowing increasingly direct, open, and respected negotiation.

Cultural norms that allow input from across an organization also allow shared leadership to flourish. Mindsets that are flexible and open to change create an environment that can adapt for creative problem-solving to handle differing and varying situations. This does not imply equal power status in every situation, but it is about capacity building for both employees and the organization as a system. The key is flexible and respectful co-leadership. Having a range of mindsets to represent conceptual, relational, analytical, and executing actions increases the opportunities for optimal success.

Voices at the Table

Boardroom decisions can be made for stockholders, whether to buy or sell entities, to change strategies or directions, where and with whom to do business; the list is endless. In both for-profit and not-for-profit companies, embedded rules are often outdated for the complex environments of the 21st century.

How are Boards of Directors accountable and responsible for the consequences of their actions? Who has a voice at the table? Boards of Directors are most often rotational with turnover neatly timed to receive bonus checks without long-term accountability for consequences of board actions. Who is charged with the well-being of employees and/or contractors?

From the penthouse view, the question to be addressed is about the gap between who owns the capital and who produces the goods and services. When does capitalism cross the line that relegates others to be less than? Embedded in my inquiry is the dignity of work. How might we honor the contributions of workers from the bottom up? The best idea in the world cannot manifest without people to create and produce goods and services. Technology is taking over mundane repetitive productions, but I do not accept that robotic or artificial intelligence can fully replicate a compassionate, competent human. Who can sit at the table with an equal voice in the equation? And to what end?

Visionaries have a predominant mindset for concepts, metaphors, and big ideas. Weavers have a predominant mindset for relating, connecting, and storytelling. Builders have a predominant mindset for constructing, mechanizing, and processing. Realists have a predominant mindset for facts, numbers, analyzing, and tracking.

Without the input of whole brain thinking, projects are not fully informed. It is easy to put people in jobs that keep role-bound behaviors as an immediate need or priority. But in highly evolving complexity, it becomes important to allow freedom for adaptability to allow workers to bring more to the equations of work. Widgets and parts can be valued as integral to the whole, not as separate. The same is true for humans

Blueprint for Shaping Your Future

who sense and see patterns and relationships of subsystems relating to the whole system and the system to its environment. Today's world can collaboratively solve root causes of problems rather than covering up symptoms that lead to dysfunction or break down.

My voice matured along with my confidence. The test came when I was working in a large corporation in the field of communications. I was given a task by the CEO to do something that I initially had doubts about. With his encouragement, I took on the assignment.

Our technical team was developing a new product that we believed would take our industry to the leading edge of possibility. One of my roles was to develop relationships with our industry trade journals to pitch story ideas. I made appointments with the two top editors. My goal was to convince each of them to save their cover story for our company six months forward in time, and the kicker was that I could not tell them anything about the story. They had to trust me that it would be worthy of their cover. The last detail was that I would not spend my budget on any advertising. It would be uncommon to have the top two industry magazines have a feature story by us in the same month.

This experience showed me the value of trust in relationships for positive outcomes with no pay for play which was the common practice. The top industry story was enough.

DuAnne Redus

Dimension III: Willingness and ability to travel new paths

Without the filter of identity, there can be no sense making and no system that can sustain itself.

—DuAnne Redus
inspired by Margaret Wheatley,
Who Do We Choose to Be?

The Yellow-Brick Road in Reverse

You can't get somewhere if you are running away or if you don't take the first step. Some of us want to stay safe no matter what. I remember the internal relief and release I felt when leaping into the abyss from the top of a 40-foot pole as a participant in a women's empowerment course. I learned what it felt like in my body to let go of patterns that were stored in my cells bound by a previously scary memory. That leap freed me to commit to myself and take other steps to continue new paths.

There are many methodologies that are useful to live a happy, fulfilled life. Some people live inside monasteries at the top of a mountain. Others live inside institutions where healthcare, education or public service creates policies and programs. There are exploratory trekking adventures and deep spiritual practices that lead to personal insight. Artisans and musicians often reveal visionary dreams. The shift from

Blueprint for Shaping Your Future

viewing work as instrumental to viewing it as sacred is a leap onto new or unknown pathways to living a fulfilled life.

The process and action of committing is one that trips up individuals and organizations on a frequent basis. Six-dimensional leaders are aware that misguided employees and coworkers will only add confusion to how work is accomplished. The right to be in the workplace is a fundamental element for long-term sustainability. People who are internally aligned with a personal value system that matches their strengths will make full-circle decisions that serve their work in whatever form it takes. The tone and tenure of personal voice becomes integrous and aligned.

Manifestation is a direct result of our focus and commitment. I have proved that concept to myself by mapping out unintended consequences too many times to name. I have learned that following the yellow brick road in reverse offers a more useful process. In my case I looked back to go forward.

Life Stages: Flip the Script

Many books have been written about stages of life. Gail Sheehy's book *Passages* was profound for me even though I had jumped over some of the predicted passages she proposed. Not everyone goes through life stages in an orderly sequential manner.

Some people have a strong will and an ability to push through phases and stages like a competition. Others start from an abandoned, confused state when

they are born and progress hesitantly. There are those who start out as frail and limited when they come out of the womb but quickly find deep inner strength.
ShaMama shows me there is no perfect or right way to begin the human journey. Every person's path is equally valid.

Amateur humans. That is how it starts. Coming into a physical body is a struggle. I remember the birthing pains from a mother's point of view. And I realize the infant has a unique experience unheard and unexplained. Some babies come out hollering and others quietly.

ShaMama says that we each choose our path when we come to this planet. Maybe we come to open hearts and minds in a family. Maybe we are here to bring shape to chaos or sift through relevant data. Maybe we come to ignite a fire. Or to soothe worried souls. There are those whose life purpose is to lift a movement toward higher ways of seeing what it means to be more authentically human. And even more of us desire to live a simple, uncomplicated life that is equally fulfilling and meaningful.

Loss, pain, fear, and uncertainty present opportunities to move beyond the habits and practice of lack and separating ourselves from what we deeply want.

I lost my way when my mother died of polio. Just two years of age, I distanced from my body as a coping skill that kept me safely away from my feelings. Disconnected from my heart, I was in limbo and

Blueprint for Shaping Your Future

isolated in my private bubble of perceived safety. I thought I had found an escape hatch living among stars, ungrounded to earth. It turned out it was only a loop that sequenced the same things over and over like the spin cycle in a washing machine. Sequencing loops are boring to me, and the essence of life pulled me back. I became a Seeker with a desire to understand how this journey we call a lifetime was relevant to me.

Was a breakout loop possible? I continuously heard a faint voice. I felt a feeling in my gut that yearned for more understanding. A sense of knowing deep inside called to me, "wake up, tune in." In time, I heard the intuitive call and stepped onto a new, unknown path. I awoke as a seeker.

As previously stated, for the sake of explicating life and work, I divide the human experience into trimesters. Birth to 30 launches us to explore. Second trimester, 31-60ish is the experiential deepening of our living. Third trimester serves up the greatest potential to synthesize and serve up our remembered wisdom.

Stand in a place of your own truth and hold the lever that is the highest expression of individual destiny.

—Jean Houston,
Archimedes Lever

DuAnne Redus

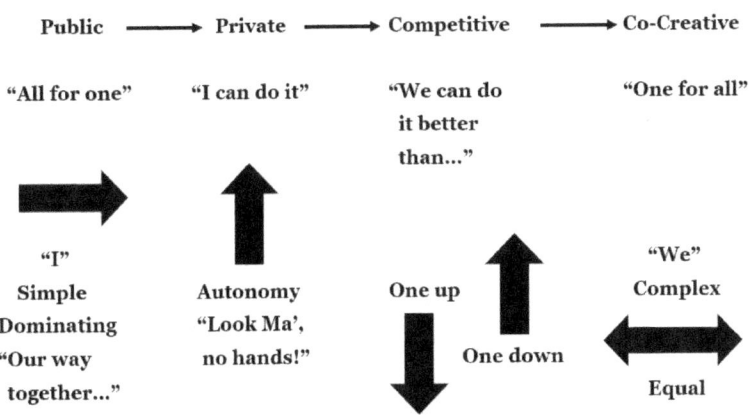

How Did I End Up Here?

"Just go to Texas and see how it works out," he coaxed. I sensed my husband was waiting to show me it wouldn't. The mental exclamations "hurry up and fail; hurry up and fail; hurry up and fail" haunted me with the continuous pulsing in my head. My body was heavy with the psychic weight of a decision I had made to leave my cushy corporate job. The consequences of making up my mind without asking for permission from my partner were like a mystery I couldn't figure out. *What is wrong with taking responsibility to make a life-turning decision that felt gut sure would lead me to a more fulfilling career and life? Quill doesn't get it!* His energy had felt heavy ever since my unexpected announcement, "I quit my job." It was excruciating to

Blueprint for Shaping Your Future

live with the suppressed, sarcastic anger seething out at me even in his sleep.

Six months later in Dallas, I sat in my seventh story office overlooking Oak Lawn Avenue at Cedar Springs waiting for my executive client to show up for her coaching session. I glanced out the window and noticed a vividly colored cardinal perched on the budding elm tree below. Instantly I was swept back home to Quill who was sick with the flu, and the circumstances that had brought me back to Texas and a big city environment.

I remembered thinking it would be easier to set up my new coaching business near a progressive city center. I thought that I would find support from my three successful and well-connected brothers. They would understand how I had beat my head against a brick wall in Utah where people lived and breathed Stephen Covey, the leadership guru.

Flashes of packing the car with a basket of audio tapes in the passenger seat next to the cooler of snacks popped in my mind. I had not laughed when Quill made jokes about sending his wife to Texas in the Lexus. The pressure felt like he was sitting and bouncing on my heart like a child with a ball trying to push out the air.

It was difficult to concentrate on what to take with me not knowing how long I'd be gone. I was up and out before the sun peeked over the Wasatch range that lines the east side of the great Salt Lake valley. I gazed at the crow's foot markings etched on the mountain I viewed every day from the front porch. "That's my mountain,"

Quill and I had quipped to each other dozens of times when we sat outside watching the sun disappear or the moon rise above the mountain crest.

My first memory of the mammoth symbol of the crow's foot marking floated through my mind. I recalled how I had believed it to be my sign to put down deep roots close to the impressive peaks. In direct conflict were the deprecating thoughts whizzing through my inner landscape at a rate I had trouble tolerating: a familiar pattern of shuffling among thoughts, feelings, and gut senses. The sniffling details about how I might not make it on my own as an independent coach and consultant fired through my neurology. An awkward, pitiful voice screamed "stop the voracious guilt that it is wrong to become strong and decisive." My heart sensed there was purpose in reaching out to the corporate world, where I had seen so many others like myself who had sold out their deepest dreams while fulfilling the need to support a family or make a living. I felt compelled to get the hell out of dodge, driving towards the mouth of the same canyon that had brought me into the valley over a decade earlier. Now I was taking the yellow brick road in reverse into the uncertainty of my future.

Distracted by anxiety, I vaguely retraced the several wrong turns I had made during the first few hours of driving. Broad daylight did nothing to shake me from the mechanical mode of moving away from both myself and my unhappy spouse. The fully loaded chariot meandered eastward as though pulled by an invisible energy over which I had no control. There was a felt

Blueprint for Shaping Your Future

sense of floating out of sync with my perception of time, space, and direction. "Is this what an out-of-body experience is like?" I had mused.

Allowing myself to stay in the fuzzy surreality gave me the freedom I was craving until I stopped twelve hours later and slept like I had been drugged. Up and out before sunrise, I was somewhere between Santa Fe and Roswell when I was stunned into present reality. The gas gauge empty light flashed fire-engine red. Avoiding reality did have its consequences.

Time to look for options. I watched for signs to get me out of this new predicament. Within a short mile or two, I spotted a ramshackle store on the side of the road. A faded blue pickup was parked in front. Pulling up beside the truck, I found myself looking into the weathered brown face of an old man. "Which way to the nearest gas pump?" I questioned. His laser black eyes drilled into mine. He didn't change his expression pointing up the highway one direction and then the opposite commenting "an hour either way." My voice barely audible, I pleaded, "but I am out of gas NOW!" Again, those penetrating eyes pierced into me as if they saw into my soul. "Follow me," he motioned. Only then did I see the small boy seated next to him. A sign of safety. Instantly, I felt guided to nod my head and accept his offer.

Driving down a nearby narrow dirt road into a small village, I quickly rolled up the car window because of the flying fine dust. The winding, rutted road could have been somewhere in Mexico where unpaved roads were common. Eventually we passed a small community church. A white cross graced the entry way over the prominent wooden door. There were no commercial establishments, only small adobe and wooden-framed homes. Time evaporated until the pickup pulled up in front of a small dwelling with a lone gas pump by the front gate. A simple shingle hung outside "Grocery". The driver pointed, waved, and drove away slowly yelling out the window, "my sister will help you."

In awe and aware of my rapidly beating heart, I got out of the car and stepped gently inside the small abode. The middle-aged Mexican woman welcomed me with a smile. "Where are you from?" She asked. "Where are you headed?" she queried further. "I'm from Salt Lake City headed to Dallas," I replied as I watched the woman's delicate body respond with hands in the air, "Well, then, how did you end up here?" We both giggled because we knew a miracle had bound the two of us, heart-to-heart.

Taps on my office door brought me back from my reminiscent journey. My client smiled and gave me a quick handshake as I opened the door and looked into the face of my new corporate client, the tangible evidence of another miracle that affirmed my decision to follow my heart's passion.

Blueprint for Shaping Your Future

Commit

My story of leaving home to navigate my path put me face to face with a choice to commit. No holdbacks. Almost would not be enough. Nearly is not yet; mostly doesn't cut it. I traded the known for the mystery and my conviction to create positive change.

Everything is a Process. Time is a construct that humans derived as environments evolved from simplistic to complex. Time itself is a paradox: past, present, future. Seasons and cycles are vivid examples. Paleolithic, Mesolithic, Neolithic ages leave their imprints. Stone age, iron age, and so on signal that more is ahead as the process continues.

Ancient wisdom teaches that the present moment is all that exists. Eastern philosophy meets western philosophy and clashes in philosophical tenets.

Connecting Global Spheres

Sundance Resort is well-known for the annual Sundance Film Festival, skiing, and lodging. Robert Redford's involvement and reputation for protecting the environment has attracted people from around the world. One of my early visions was to host an executive retreat at the facility, called *Connecting Global Spheres*, with the connotations of connection, bridging physical geography, and linking the double-sided brain.

We invited guest speaker Peter Russell, a thought leader in the early 1990s whose books, *The Global Brain* and *The Global Brain Awakens* had ignited forward thinking all around the world. Somehow, I managed to get his phone number, and when I called, he answered the phone. Surprised, I made the request and he accepted!

Peter was soft-spoken, gentle and brilliant. His concepts about human connection on a global scale were mind opening.

Two decades later I realize how much his influence stimulated my thinking about personal potential and jumpstarted a new career path. Much of my potential was latent but the sparks continued to burst into creative acts as I began to grow from an unaware human into an awakening human.

Once again, the thought "when we are ready a teacher/mentor/guide appears often disguised or unrecognizable to our rational brain!" ShaMama is my best example as I have continued to speak the voice she represents, when I choose to listen.

One of the experiences Peter gave us was to sit in silence. It was obvious how uncomfortable and unnerving this seemingly simple task was to us all. Unaccustomed to slowing down as executives, the concept of stillness was uncommon. In today's world during the long pause of a pandemic, it seems the entire globe has gained the unexpected and valuable gifts of slowing down and time to sit in stillness and reflection. We still need more practice!

Business paradigms that freeze organizational cultures in time continue to evolve. My life's work has been to defrost the models of "right to work" towards a "right to be." The desire to contribute is imbued in most

Blueprint for Shaping Your Future

humans. Work to earn an income is on the verge of a cultural shift to the concept of being valued for who we are and what we have to offer. The COVID pandemic caused businesses of all sizes and shapes to re-evaluate how work can happen. Working from home achieved a higher value for many. For others with children, work took on an added dimension of more work as they became home schoolers. And for the front-line workers, lives took on higher risks as they were forced into unsafe environments. There are circumstances that sometimes converge in ways that create an opening for regeneration. Re-identifying our collective beliefs and values presents the opportunity to raise the awareness of who we are together and what we can accomplish.

A Change of Plans

I have sat through thousands of hours with groups to develop plans for the future of organizations, both as a participant and as a facilitator. It is not that I am against planning. But there is a pattern I noticed about people who are often in charge of planning. They are not prepared! Prepared? I saw a lack of commitment to "the" plan. Mainly, the task of planning was a form of busy work to be checked off a list and put on a shelf.

True preparation requires more. What does it mean to get real buy-in? The process and action of committing often trips up individuals and organizations. Unless a plan becomes a flexible blueprint, it is more like a relic than a road map. Preparing is about the people who oversee executing a strategy. That's where to begin. Without consensus from the "we," plans are insignificant.

When group experiences about planning have proven to be ineffective multiple times, the belief becomes negative about the need to have a concrete plan. If I believe I am a minion in the scheme of work, that filter will compromise how I value my contribution, and whether I even want to positively contribute. Identity is the filter that makes sense of our reality. Am I a minion or valued contributor? Maybe the wake-up call is to recognize which I choose to be in my domain of working.

A Teaching Intervention

One day I was in the UK supporting some newer members of our training team. Connor was facilitating a leadership development group and I tagged along as his coach. He was an exuberant facilitator with a lean, tall frame well over six feet. As he spoke, he began to move closer to the seated participants. My perspective from the sidelines was of a monster looming over his prey. From my observer point of view, I noticed that listeners began to change their body language as heads went down and shoulders slumped. It was as if all energy had been vacuumed from the room. Conner was losing the attention of the group and consequent ability to hear what he was saying. The connection broke.

Rather than let the situation decompose further, I stood up and walked over to Conner physically leaning against him with my arms crossed until he was slightly off-balance. Laughter filled the room with a sense of relief. Not understanding, Connor looked at me with a question mark signaled by his hands. What? I just smiled and walked back to my observer mode.

At dinner the same evening, Connor began probing about my seemingly strange interruption. What was that about? We discussed the teaching moment of which he had been unaware. He learned that his physical presence could be perceived as a threat. The next day in class he chose to sit in a chair as he addressed the group so as not to tower above them. I explained I had demonstrated a tiny intervention rather than watch him lose trust with the participants.

Subtleties, nuances, and circumstances offer the ability to bridge instead of separate. Embracing these moments in our lives, we begin to understand unseen opportunities that sometimes show up internally or externally. Connor gained inner awareness in relationship to his environment.

The Castle

During my years of extensive travel with transformational organizational work, I was privileged to be part of a project in Scotland. Planes, trains, and car rides from the U.S. produced a tired traveler. Every project gave me a new opportunity. There was never a sure outcome and no set plan for each event with hundreds of groups. Mystery prevailed as I maneuvered through varying cultural circumstances and dozens of groups.

My sleep was disturbed in unexpected ways the first night I spent in the castle converted to a hotel and conference venue on the outskirts of Edinburgh. Exhausted, I expected to fall asleep quickly. But something felt off. Voices in my head. Screaming women's voices. *What? Hallucinations, dreams, nightmares?*

Next morning at breakfast I inquired about the history of the castle. My heart skipped a beat when I was told the castle had once been a place where convicted witches had been burned at the stake. There was no rational explanation for the energetic nuances I had perceived in present time as I bumped into the past verified by historical facts. A hint of tortured souls. We've heard that walls have ears, right? Maybe walls even have a voice?

Shaken. I want outside to find solace walking toward the magnificent symmetrical trees surrounding the premises. The pathways took me away from the stark reality I had learned about the castle's long forgotten history. One foot in front of the other, my eyes raised toward the grey sky. Soon I came upon what looked like a giant mound of earth at least 25 feet in diameter and two feet in height. Curious, I approached to see that it was a circular earthen structure. Coming closer, I could see there were etched patterns carved within the compacted dirt. Later I found out that the sketches were war game strategies that had been mapped upon the now fossilized surface. Deliberately drawn. I was touched again by a history that continues beyond what is obvious to the senses.

Blueprint for Shaping Your Future

Intuitively I turned and walked counterclockwise around the molded earth structure. Around and around, I went, as if unwinding time, envisioning healing for the place and all the secrets it embodied. Finally, I felt grounded and ready for the day. The information I had gained gave me insight into the history of a people and place that lifted my appreciation for the group waiting in the castle.

Once again, ShaMama, the Wisdom Keeper, affirmed my intuitive knowing of things unseen. In my head I didn't fully understand my experience. My heart had been touched by the invisible vibes of the place, and my gut knew I could trust my intuitive insight.

DuAnne Redus

© Tichonj

Warrior Spirits

I am standing in an oval-shaped room in the Scottish castle. Repurposed as a venue, it is stunning to see remnants of the original structure. Fifteen men are sitting with me in this rock-walled ancient room. It's surreal. Sensing their slight bewilderment about what they were doing here with a small-boned, short, quiet-voiced woman from the United States, I question myself, "what am I doing in a castle in Scotland?"

This is where we begin. The heavy brough dialect makes it difficult for me to understand and translate their words and names. I finally request they speak only

Blueprint for Shaping Your Future

if I can read their lips, and not while I'm scribing on the whiteboard! Certainly, they have the same request of me with my Texas dialect. Bodies begin to settle in.

Suddenly, I look around the room and blurt, "I do not know how I got here! How did this girl who grew up in Texas get the opportunity to be with you?" Relief. The spell of discomfort among us is broken. Vulnerable, we move forward slowly and carefully together. The material comes alive when I become the conduit and not the teacher. We begin: "What does a modern-day leader look like?"

Time for a personal introduction. Still tender from the death of my husband, my story revealed how his unexpected passing had allowed me to get in touch with a deeper me.

Quill, sometimes known to his staff as Atilla the Hun, was a Warrior from the touchstone of having been a commissioned officer in the Marines after college during the Viet Nam War. He led his team as an executive in the corporate world with humor and a sense of power I did not understand. Every task he performed was accomplished with fervor. Even picking peaches from our backyard tree, I could feel the force field of his energy as I became more capable of sensing certain vibes.

Unconsciously, I was in constant longing for him to transform into something more palatable to me. "Why can't you be less fierce and tame your energy?" seeped into my conscious thoughts. Over time my internal perception of him caused palpable disconnections in our relationship. I could feel myself repel his actions that I defined as harsh. "What is important to understand," I explained to the room of Scots, "is that I was unaware of how powerful my thoughts were. Unaware."

Desperate to mend our fracturing relationship, my heart told my head that it was my problem, not his. ShaMama's voice whispered to me. I decided to spend a day at the public library researching warriors. How had I become so disdainful? Through time warriors were important, needed, and respected. As I read through dozens of books about various kinds of warriors, I chose words that described the benefits, characteristics and energies that resonated within me. Protectors, Providers, Chivalrous Knights, Samurai, Ninjas, Maori Chiefs. Disciplined, honorable, equipped, organized, and committed were characteristics I admired. Surprised, I learned that the word *kamikaze* is defined as "divine wind" in Japanese. My list was long as I made notes and gained a wider appreciation for warriors. In the purest form, as a warrior learns to be sensitive to the environs; he/she finds the timing to intervene respectfully. The warrior waits and is sensitive to openings. The challenge of the warrior is to gain the power of energy-in-motion, also known as emotion. Warriors assess the energy of the present and bring appropriate energy to a situation. It could be passion, or perhaps compassion. In the past, these sensitivities were for survival. In today's complicated environments, these senses are to bring additive energy, far beyond survival.

Blueprint for Shaping Your Future

The list changed my perspective about my husband. I meditated and tucked the positive uplifting new thoughts into my heart, holding them close. Although Quill never knew what I had done, our relationship was mended. Our energies meshed. Previously perceived competition between us evaporated. We became partners, equally valid.

When he died unexpectedly at home while I was travelling on business, the day before his fifty-second birthday, I was shaken to my core. How could I move on with no back up, without my partner? We were not financially prepared. It occurred to me that I might need to get a regular job, which was something I had discarded with abandon years before when I left my "safe" corporate job. I was facing another unfamiliar path.

Unbeknownst to me at that point, my sense of identity had expanded. I recognized that I had been presented with the gift of claiming my own Warrior archetype, one I had previously distained. Another dormant seed began to blossom, another counterpart to ShaMama. My new situation as a young widow allowed me to claim strengths I had previously shunned. More integration began to give me additional internal resources that I could draw upon as needed.

My fellow participants in the castle began to unravel more of their own personal identities.

DuAnne Redus

A continuous desire to learn and explore various cultures presented me with my next adventure. Invited to go to Peru, I became immersed in an environment high in the Andes. Another mysterious path had been revealed.

		Timeframes		
Agricultural →	Industrial →	Information →	Knowledge →	Wisdom 21st Century
Dependency for the good of the farm	Independence Autonomous	Competitive Us vs. Them	Interdependent Partnering / Co-operative Collaborative	Interdependent Co-creative Alignment

Blueprint for Shaping Your Future

Dimension IV: Willingness and ability to face conflict and paradox

The curious paradox is that when I accept myself just as I am, then I can change.

—Carl R. Rogers,
On Becoming a Person:
A Therapist's View of Psychotherapy

A jolting revelation shook me when I was well into my second trimester between 30 and 60 years of age. I was shocked when I discovered the reality of how much I had trusted others instead of trusting myself. Consequently, I had carried my *not trusting myself* everywhere I went: social circles, family relationships and work. The shift in the perception that I did not know how to trust myself, led me to another internal junction.

Trust or Fear

Trust is at the core of well-being. We always have a choice to trust or to fear. Fear raises our defensive behaviors. Period. Fear sends signals that alienate. Hostility boils inside. "I am alone" flows through our veins. The antidote for fear is to physically notice the present moment. Feel your body, adjust your internal barometer, reframe the scary thought!

Naturally, there are times when fear is a signal that informs positively. But that is not the fear that entraps us in daily living. Think of a continuum that allows the "trust meter" to increase at will. The tendrils of distrust seep into the domains of work, community, or government.

It became apparent that my mistrust was more about me and the underlying assumptions that led me to examine who and what outside myself was trustworthy. I had learned to hold my emotions at bay. One might say I stuffed my feelings deep in my gut. There is a junction at which our "experience of self" and our "familiarity of self" meet. Somewhere in the mix is a jumble in which of our senses of taste, smell, hearing, seeing and intuiting are attached to remembered experiences. The senses create imprints that may be negative and sideline how we trust. This is another instance when we may need to do some truth-busting.

My increasing ability to tune in and remember many of my sleep dreams has been impactful to my life. Journaling tidbits recalled from night dreams, intertwined with my daily writing, has helped to bridge my conscious and other-than-conscious reality. The information I receive and interpret gives me useful guidance in my living experience and goes into my memory bank. I have discovered symbols and images unique to me, not necessarily defined or generalized in the collective past. Interpretations of symbols evolve to align with current context.

A life dilemma showed itself to me on a cold winter's night in my dream world: I am standing at the

Blueprint for Shaping Your Future

bottom of a deep and narrow crevasse. The ravine's steep walls are cold, bumpy, and rough. My eyes adjust as I gaze up the right side of the wall. I look up, up, up. I focus closely, determined to quickly find a way out. Surprised, I see a barbed wire fence at the top with armed guards peering downward as if searching to see me. My inner voice screams, "No! No! No!" I pull inward and sit on the hard earth. After a short while I gather my courage. I stand and look again. I allow my eyes to be softer as I gaze upwards to the left side of the ravine, attempting to manage my fear.

My inner voice calmly speaks to me: "It's okay, keep looking." At the crest I see the amber eyes of a large puma peering directly into my eyes with the intensity of a laser beam. "Come, come, come! I will show you the way." The magnetic energy is peaceful. My heart seems to be penetrated with a sense of courage and curiosity. Intuitively, I accept the message attracting me towards the raw, undomesticated energy. My resolve is strengthened by taking deep, slow breaths. I begin to climb carefully up the steep ascent.

Although it would seem a paradox to move towards untamed energy, the large cat was more appealing than facing prison guards who were likely to incarcerate me. Once again, I had trusted myself to choose, and the puma had become a positive figure in my symbolic dictionary connoting an animating force of mystery that, although uncertain, was not scary.

DuAnne Redus

© Libux77

Conflict in the Workplace

For a moment, let's imagine a workplace filled with people who lack the sense of trust. Is my boss really looking out for my best interest? Is my team working collaboratively or as individuals only looking out for themselves? Is the company focused on quarterly financial goals instead of long-range sustainability? Is this truly a place I can rely upon to support my contributions?

People who are trustworthy to uphold personal values are more reliable. Reciprocity is a two-way process. Employees and workers deserve respect and dignity and are not minions to be used as parts that can be easily replaced.

Blueprint for Shaping Your Future

In tandem to lack of self-belief, the prevailing identity of any organization sets the structure for the rules, roles and relationships. Underlying assumptions permeate the cultural environment and can set up conflict, dilemmas and paradox. Our task was to find ways to align with clarity, trust, and resourcefulness.

It became apparent to me working with leaders in organizations that ethics, morals, and values most often did not line up well between the people and the structures. Unspoken or disavowed rules often dominated decision-making processes. An invisible network sometimes blurred the line between what was or was not accepted as appropriate behaviors. Gossip, backstabbing, competitive manipulation, glad-handing, and lack of trust manifest like wildfires, especially during cycles of change or stagnation.

Ethics are how we decide to behave when we decide to work together. The question becomes, "how do we relate with others given cultural nuances?"

If I am unsure about my core values, morals, and ethics, how will I trust my decisions, especially when I'm expected to align with opposing expectations? My belief is that when I live from my authentic identity, the essential self, I will become choosy about where, with whom and how I decide what making a living means to me. Making a living often seems like something we must do, instead of what we want to do. I found it to be true as a single mother with three children. The corporate world offered me a steady pathway, for which I am grateful. When my youngest child graduated from college, a choice presented itself: "Am I willing to continue to play the game that puts profit over people?" I chose to leave that environment, trusting myself to find a way to sustain myself.

I could have stayed, distanced myself from my inner longing, and continued to accept the hearty paycheck. From my place in the organization, changing the culture was not an option. Leaving was risky, but I could see the possibility of a new path that made my heart jump with eagerness. I sought to thrive, rather than stay safe and unfulfilled. I continued to sort and sift until my creative juices began to align with my dedication to creating collaborative relationships in my work. There was no blame that the company failed me. I just wanted something else.

What are the questions to ask when interviewing a company or an organization to become an employee? We can flip the script, in effect giving messages to businesses that we expect to be treated fairly and equitably. Can we see evidence of transparency? What kind of culture will be supported towards a path with opportunity for personal growth, skill development or a new career?

If we take a penthouse view of the world of work, it follows that the top floor has the widest view and opportunities. The basement or ground-level view shows a story of the worker bees who are necessary for perpetuating life at the top. There is nothing wrong with living at the top, bottom or in-between if all are respected and valued with equanimity. Today's world, however, values money and power over humanity and equanimity. The drivers of economies are supported by business models which are weighted unfairly by valuing capital over labor. This causes distrust in the labor force.

Nothing Fails Like Success

In evolution, the saying that nothing fails like success is probably always right. A creature which has become perfectly adapted to the environment, an animal whose whole capacity and vital force is concentrated and expanded in succeeding here and now, has nothing left over with which to respond to any radical change. Age by age, it becomes more perfectly economical in the way its entire resources meet exactly its current and customary opportunities. In the end it can do all that is necessary to survive without any conscious striving or unadoptive movement.

—Arnold Toynbee

The example that comes to mind is an economy that measures gross domestic and gross national product which is based on a formula for production and consumption. According to some experts, GDP was not designed to determine material well-being, but rather serves as an indicator of the country's productivity. On an annual basis it measures output and consumer spending. The system is based on funding the government without measuring the consequences to people.

Selling sugar and tobacco are great for GDP and GNP, but do not consider the harmful costs of health. What is not counted as production is the hard work of people who care for children, the elderly and other at-home care.

Unfortunately, the system leaves out the indicators of what is good for the people and the planet. Trickle-down economics is a cover up that exploits the relationship between budgeting and government deficits. The current economic system does not work the way our household budget works. A successful economy has been defined in a manner that is out of date with the human side of measurements.

Modern monetary theory, along with other progressive models, presents alternative formulas that consider cultural transformation. A narrative that moves beyond if/then, cause and effect, to terms of interactive processes, is more realistic for complex systems.

The history of domination systems, with their inherent exploitation of people and nature, social and economic inequities, and direct and structural violence, are evident worldwide.

During the pandemic that began in 2020, it became obvious what is not counted in our current economy. Many were left out of the calculation that creates a fair, thriving economy that is good for the many, not the few. The Center for Partnership Studies developed "Social Wealth Economic Indicators" that go beyond GDP to include environmental conditions as well as levels of health, education, and poverty. This is one hopeful example of pressure for increasing corporate accountability that takes unintended consequences into account in the development of products and services.

The Law of Requisite Variety

In any system, the element with the most flexibility will have the most influence over that system. The more different results you want, the more variety is needed. For example, when a competitive environment pushes an organization to its limits, the old mindset no longer holds. Continuous improvement in capability and how we think is needed, and that involves expanding our ways to think as a system that includes long-term consequences.

The companies that thrive in fast-changing environments are flexible to make quick changes, and have workers who willingly adapt to alternative processes and methods as a way of doing business. Restaurants who were not hesitant to pivot from inside dining to outside or take-away meals during the pandemic demonstrated resilience. More examples are evident, like the companies who created the coronavirus vaccine through multi-national collaboration on a timeline that was incredulous. Tesla has long-view sensibility. NASA dwells in present time and prepares for future time. Biotechnology is delving into unknown territory to enable physical healing that was once thought impossible. Companies that continue their reliance on fossil fuels in the future will become extinct as sustainable alternatives increase. Some energy companies are moving towards wind and solar, which do not depend on extracting resources from our planet.

The common ground among us is that our mindsets need an upgrade so that we can navigate the complexities of paradox, conflict, dilemmas, and uncertainty. A tendency exists in the misdirected understanding of time that we want to leap over to some other side of reality without sitting in the present long enough to connect to threads of wisdom.

Morphing archetypes are evolving symbols that demonstrate the collaborations needed as we widen our collective identities. Partnership, Eldership, Sustainability Coaches, and Confidence Supporters connote sharing and caring. Are we only a collection of rugged individualists seeking self-interest? Are we becoming a collection of distinguishable gems who collaborate for common good? How can we use our collective mindsets for the many? In every crisis it is the collective mindset that sustains and carries us to the other side. Not one person has power to do it alone. Global citizens realize it is imperative to do no harm, and that requires patience, connection and understanding.

Where are we going; who is going with us; how do we get there, and how do we recalibrate to stay on track or add a track? We need an on-going process that includes all of us. How do we create environments that allow inquiry, creativity, passion, truth-telling and critical thinking without fear of retribution? Structures, patterns, and cycles inform the overall health of a system. Seeing the connections leads to better solutions.

My personal experience mentioned in the boardroom story gave me the opportunity to acknowledge that my corporate job was limiting me as someone with untapped potential. I was forced to accept or deny what was true for me. I allowed myself to deepen my self-trust over perceptions others had of me. I stayed in that newly imagined space long enough for new options to show themselves. There was not a preplanned course of action. I recognized that my skill development over 21 years had given me additional competencies and capacity. I had learned to trust myself within a system.

Ripples in Life

Ripples of confusion spread throughout my life as I gained more self-trust. My husband was scared I would fail. He held on more tightly to his 'safe' corporate job for security. Although his resistance was problematic for our relationship, I persevered into unknown territory. We agreed on a timeline to allow me the chance to succeed. If it didn't work out, I agreed to take a job at an executive placement firm from which I had been offered an opportunity as a recruiter.

As a consultant, I remember my first contract with an accounting software company that blossomed into a three-year project. After searching for people whose values and vision were compatible with mine, our collaboration took me deeper into a sense of confidence and accomplishment. My focus and commitment had manifested a different career that led me to international work with an even more diverse collaboration.

In the meantime, unforeseen circumstances happened. My husband was given a severance package from his company. He was thrust into an unknown situation and had to re-identify himself and his profession. His field in corporate contracts over many years had given him a niche he self-identified as "the junkyard dog," finding solutions without a map. Through coaching, he discovered the limitations of that identifier. When he was able to claim his value as "the seeker of treasures," his confidence increased with the possibility that he would find a more suitable way forward towards retirement.

He left me a note one day as he left for interviews in another state:

"Du, I watered the plants. Off to see the Wizard. Maybe I'll find something there. Love, Dorothy."

Elated by his sense of humor and hope, I had no idea how that short statement would affect our lives.

His energy lightened up as a treasure-seeker by planning a surprise cruise for us. We embarked on a jazz cruise with intimate performances each night. Our last adventure together was filled with cherished memories. He died six months later. The note he had written to me became the centerpiece of his memorial celebration.

Blueprint for Shaping Your Future

Once more, I was living in a state of ambiguity. Was I capable and did I believe strongly enough that I could stay on the path of my heart, or would it be better to go back to the perceived security of being an executive recruiter? Sitting in pain and loss, I made the decision to stay on my path. The thoughts in my head went through more truth-busting. "There's no such thing as security in a job," I accepted as my truth. My heart lined up with that belief because I received so much joy from the work I was engaged with. Once again, I trusted my gut. My commitment was to show up 100% for myself. I was reminded about my sleep dream looking up the ravine into the eyes of the wild puma. Paradox stared me down, and yet I made a choice supported by my deep values to be unbounded by trust.

Embedded assumptions hold organizations static. As an example of more simplistic organizing structures, I refer to a Yukon tribe of the Pacific Northwest, who lived in a narrow river valley. They deduced that the ellipse of about 150 miles in diameter included all there was in the world. There was no east, south, west, north. There was only upstream, downstream, toward the river and away from the river. All decisions were based on these assumptions in a time-binding process. In contrast, the world of the Sioux tribes as hunters roamed the plains and cultivated spatial concepts that included horizons and mobility. Boundaries changed consistently; the concept of storage over prolonged time was foreign to them. They placed emphasis on the "give away" and trading essentials on their next stop.

Organizational Paradigms

My team of consultants observed similar narrow structures within our client organizations. Early in our projects we saw four main metaphorical patterns:

Family: The patriarch/father will take care of us; mother will take care of us (obedient)

Military: We will protect you and keep you safe requiring loyalty (double bind) (submissive)

Sports: Winners over losers, binary; either/or (competitive)

Technology: We have the/your answers (blind trust)

Coming from an exploratory point of view that the organizations had their own answers; we were there to set a stage for what was not seen or understood by their frozen structures. We examined alternative organizing patterns, such as ones that mirrored nature, or the science of self-organizing systems and metaphors that embody tenets of well-being and wholeness.

Blueprint for Shaping Your Future

The metaphor of jazz is one of my favorite organizing structures, implying that music can be created in a jam session where many instruments come in and out of the whole, each playing their individually crafted art in the moment. There is no one way. The music can meander, climax, turn a rhythm. It is experiential for each participant skilled in their instrument, willing to blend, stand out, step in and out to highlight others. Sensory and sensing.

© Charithain4

Competencies of individuals in organizations are many. The relationship between competence and style touches on how leaders behave. Optimally, capable negotiation, individual choice, and the ability to consider ambiguity are developed in all people. Style respects demonstrating the warmth, presence and humor that are relevant to the context of a situation. The current landscapes of complexity require the ability to understand when we get caught in double-binds, paradoxical situations and dilemmas which are traps that can be avoided and escaped. Describing a concept is distinctively different from the experience!

What is a double bind? Dictionaries define it as a situation in which a person is confronted with two irreconcilable demands or a choice between two undesirable outcomes (New Oxford American Dictionary).

What is paradox? It is defined as a seemingly absurd or self-contradictory statement or proposition that when investigated or explained may prove to be well founded or true (New Oxford American Dictionary).

Dilemmas occur in communications when we tell children they are creative, but when they paint on the living room wall they are shamed. Structures within organizations often reward the high achievers with pay while punishing the steady-minded process thinkers. Double binds are often used as a form of control. Triangulation in relationships sets up manipulative tactics. Two people in conflict often seek a third who can be caught in a web of deceit and conflicting points of view.

Polarities exist in our definitions, actions, and consequences of life. Demonstrating this concept in a group setting, the participants gained awareness of how polarities can cause division. We placed long sheets of butcher paper on the floor lengthwise in the training room. On one end of the paper was written POWER,

Blueprint for Shaping Your Future

and on the opposite end was written PEACE. The group was divided in half and tasked to write individual definitions of the word on the paper. Words described peace as calm, passive, soft, tranquil, without war, non-violent, inner compass, stress-free, harmony, free, powerful, fulfilling. Participants described power as strong, powerful, forceful, inner confidence, overly influential, physical, inner power, authoritative, militaristic, free.

Then the two groups changed places to review the definitions previously scribed on the floor. The ensuing conversation revealed how differently each word was perceived by their peers. They began to discuss how they might not accurately understand one another without more curiosity and discovery. They concluded that listening and probing could be useful to them, not only as co-workers, but also with their clients and customers. The participants were left with thoughts to ponder: *Can there be power in peace? Can there be peace in power?*

My mentor, Marj Barlow, Ph.D. once told me that the opposite of old is not young. In her mind, the opposite of old is new! I laughed at how easily she had influenced my inner map. Our brains, hearts and intuitions are systems within systems that are unhealthy or healthy, aligned or misaligned, tuned-in or tuned-out!

Spectrum of Truth

Let's explore the concepts of truth. Truth is always only "partial." Splinters of truth show up everywhere. There is my truth, your truth, and a higher truth. Where do we start?

1. If we consider truth as a process, i.e., "truing," perhaps we will be more inclined to stretch the definition. Carpenters have a tool at their disposal to find the "through line" in a piece of wood or stone. I saw evidence of this in Peru in the large stone structures built in the Andes before the Spaniards conquered the Inca. Craftsmen could see the line that helped split monumental-sized granite into building blocks with small hand tools.
2. Reality includes the unreal and untrue. Our perceptions distort the information according to our conditioning and the degree of our focus and internal motivation.
3. My map of reality is as valid as your map of reality whether similar, different, or opposite.

Discerning truth is a process that is sometimes internal and often external.

It is true that my father was known to be a fabulous dancer. He could navigate a ballroom waltzing, foxtrotting, or jitterbugging around the floor. He also had rhythm. Latin, blues, or classic, he felt music in his bones. I claim to have inherited his love of music and dance. Often, I dance when nobody else is dancing, as they say, to the beat of my own drum. The gypsy avatar in me is infatuated with dance!

Blueprint for Shaping Your Future

It is also true that I did not know how to dance the way my father could dance until I learned the steps. Feeling the vibe did not always mesh with the skill my partner used to fling and dip and swirl me around the dance floor.

Organizations have a signature vibe, skill set and idea of the future. Friction rubs against the grain when there is no communication about the playlist, how to prepare or where the dance is. Remember what it was like to stand on the sidelines of your first high school dance, with no partner in sight? Or to be hesitant to ask a partner to dance? Who did you later wish you had invited? What was it like in your first professional job or contract? Did you have a method to discern what was happening below the surface within the organization?

It is useful to remember that people show up to work as young, maybe immature workers even if they have earned their degrees and checked all the boxes in an interview. Others show up pretending they know, don't need to ask and fumble finding their way. And of course, mature, skilled, and aware people also enter the workforce.

Without internal navigational bearings, how can we possibly find out where we fit and what we have to offer to the idea of making a living without burning ourselves out by the time we enter our second trimester of life?

Naturally, our skills increase along the way and our confidence builds. We find out more about what energizes and pulls us forward as well as the things that drain our energy with no replenishment.

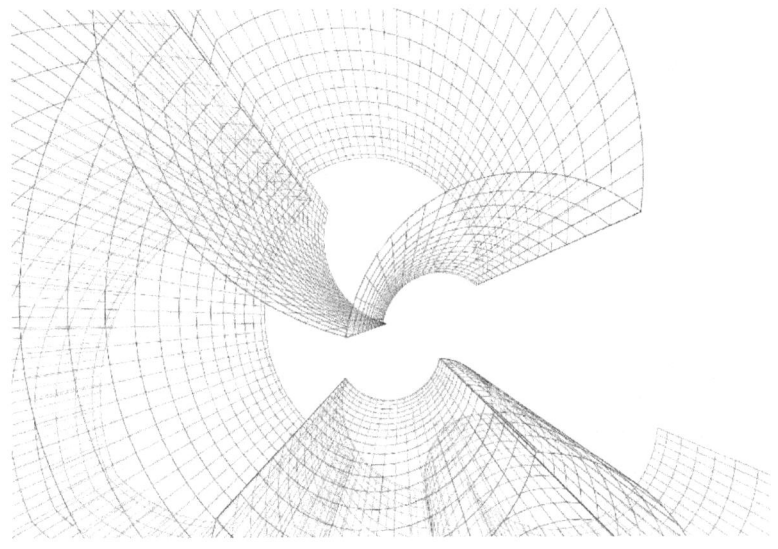

© Sofiya Kavalchuk

The process of "truing" with the essence of who we are, is one solution to align with the "right to be" paradigm in work and life. Paradoxes and conflicts merge as we accept higher versions of truth. My inner conflict about warriors merged with my identity when I claimed the inherent resources of the warrior.

Blueprint for Shaping Your Future

Dimension V: Willingness and ability to bridge relationships in family, work, community.

Each individual inherits a collective memory from past members of the species, and contributes to the collective memory, affecting other members of the species in the future. We have a projection of the whole to constitute a moment; a moment is a movement.

—Rupert Sheldrake, Ph.D.

Morphic Resonance

Rupert Sheldrake introduced the idea of morphic resonance from his studies of biology. Not knowing about the concept way back in 1981, I sensed this concept relating to wisdom long before I had a way to explain it. The next story tells how experience has invisible teachings.

As a young child I became deathly afraid of spiders when I was cornered on the patio by a large tarantula. In my reality that spider was bigger than an octopus. The fear stayed with me into young adulthood. Any spider I encountered carried the stigma into the present moment.

It's no wonder, Grandmother Spider appeared to me when I lived near the four-corners area of Utah, New Mexico, Arizona, and Colorado in the

Southwestern United States. The Legacy of Spider Woman prevails in the traditions of the Navajo and Hopi. The long-lived oral tradition was told to me when I visited Spider Rock, the 800-foot-tall formation in Canyon de Chelly.

Spider Woman, grandmother of Earth and all life, holds concern and focus for all peoples. She is the preserver of life, the weaver of webs, a mentor and helper to those who ask. She creates a central source to weave the web of life. She is the essence of patience. She holds the tension between holding on and letting go. She lets things unfold naturally in their own time.

The Hopi story of Grandmother Spider tells of how she assists those who seek meaning and truth. She is summoned to go to all creatures to help them move on. After the Great Sun Spirit created the lower world, it became apparent there was so much more. Great Sun Spirit called Grandmother Spider.

She appeared. One of her first tasks was to lead the people to ascend into the next world above the lower world, where the light was dim and cold. After a period of getting along together in the underworld, the people began to yearn for more. They wanted more choices and ways to move on. Their strong intentions took them higher, to the doorway of the upper world.

Grandmother Spider appeared with her young warrior and great godsons. They planted seeds that could grow tall and upward. Grandmother Spider urged all to sing without stopping to assist the sprouting and bursting forth of the seeds. She urged all who wanted to

Blueprint for Shaping Your Future

go through the doorway to the sky to ponder deeply before they entered the opening to begin the journey to become true humans.

They ascended into a new place where Grandmother Spider showed them how to bring light and warmth into the world. Then she put a lake over the hole through which they had come and told the people to carefully prepare. "Only those who forget why they came to this world will lose their way," she admonished. "It is one thing to cope with your new life but quite another to let it unfold." My understanding of this wisdom in parallel with present time is relevant today. I busted through my fear of spiders. The myth relates to gaining awareness according to the willingness to see. Spiders have purpose.

Many years later, when my work took me to northern England, I saw the beauty of weaving on a walk through a field. The early morning sun shone on plants kissed by dew. My eyes caught the image of fragile webs woven in the night hours across the tops of plants. I literally saw the web of life reflecting soft sunlight, and I thanked Grandmother Spider for an intimate view of life-connecting patterns.

Wisdom seeps from the bones. It connotes a sense of meaning that surpasses information and knowledge easily gained at the tip of a finger on the worldwide web. What is the wisdom from the ancients that wants to be remembered and carried into the presence of Now? It depends on the translation. Who are the ones willing and capable of bringing forth the deep meaning of wisdom from ancestors? Story weavers are chosen via links and bridges of the invisible who carry forth wisdom. Universal truths are often held in carefully crafted oral traditions.

Ancestral Wisdom
Past and future points experienced in present time.

You are the fairy tale told by your ancestors.

—Toba Beta
My Ancestor Was an Ancient Astronaut

Who did I come here to be? For me, this crosses the intersections of time. When I read various scientific theories, my sense of time changed once more. The fifth dimension is an inner space where archetypes, the past, present, and future converge. It is my experience although it is difficult to explain. It has much to do with how I identify myself to myself. The more I was able to embody a particular archetype or avatar, I gained more of my internal superpowers connected to threads of wisdom in the ethers. My intuition was more accurate as a pathway to truth, than the things I saw in the material world. Not in a foreseeing way, but in a way that I connected with my inner sensibilities.

Change comes from releasing the appropriate resource or activating the potential resource for a particular context by enriching our personal map of the world. Each of my 12 personal archetypes have shown me inner keys to connect to resources as needed.

Blueprint for Shaping Your Future

Resources that had been latent, dormant, and unknown to me. Each archetype connects the past, present, and future into a web of wisdom from which I can relate to in any context when I notice.

When I learned about fractals years ago, it became a game to see patterns within patterns. Nature was my first subject matter to explore. Information re-patterned is sometimes obvious and often not so obvious. I use the mandala of my archetypes as my identity map. My expanded identity of metaphors is integral to who I am becoming, just as the universe is connected to other galaxies and yet whole as an entity. Leaders who see, connect and re-orient to embedded patterns within their organizations are wise to notice!

Ritual, celebration, and playfulness are requisite to becoming more fully human. All cultures have distinctive definitions that expand or limit these concepts held in their collective identities. An ancient Indonesian ritual demonstrates the wholeness of a human in a dance where the males/females adorn an elaborate costume of their opposite gender's inner characteristic thus integrating both into their essence as a being.

Collective celebrations raise the energetic vibration of joy and fulfillment. New ways to celebrate birth and death are merging. Revealing the gender of a child in utero in fun ways links generations awaiting a birth. The memorial of life service is becoming a more popular way to release a loved one. In addition to religious church services, outdoor events can incorporate nature. Green burials are sought to regenerate and not contaminate the earth with embalming fluids that are toxic. Human composting may become popular in the future!

Long gone are the 25-year gold watch awards given to loyal employees. People are likely to have five to seven career changes in modern times signaling mobility and adaptability for workers as the 21st Century unfolds. Less commuting to workplaces is evident with increasing technological and communication tools. Homeschooling is trending across the USA as the risk of biological virus mutations creep around the world. Connectivity between cultures via global outreach increases the recognition for egalitarian solutions for health and well-being. Leaders are discovering that social skills are highly rated in all domains of work.

Rupert's research in morphic resonance explicated characteristics of self-organizing wholes, aspects of space and time, attractor energies that influence others, along with the concept that there are built-in memories that when often repeated become more habitual. He demonstrated that the fields of our minds extend far beyond our brains.

Increasing the human capacities for tolerance, respect and care is a fundamental prerequisite to creating a world to which we all want to belong. Without a sense of self-concept, there is no organizing process. When we separate our work from the rest of our life, breakdowns occur frequently and systematically.

Blueprint for Shaping Your Future

Bridges connect and bind us together. They can be gateways to discover something new or look back to the past. Simple footbridges, functional toll bridges or stunning works of art are among the multiple choices.

Structurally sound bridges are well known. The London Bridge spans River Thames in London, the London Bridge over Lake Havasu in Arizona, the Brooklyn Bridge in New York, and the Golden Gate Bridge in San Francisco are examples of massive-sized structures. Suspension bridges, trestle bridges and through-gate bridges are designed to meet environmental challenges.

I once crawled over a fallen tree that was crossing a river on a hiking adventure because others went ahead of me. I began to consider bridging relationships that needed mending or developing. Pedestrian bridges show up in curious places. A hand-made rope bridge across a ravine was the most challenging for me to use. There was no underpinning structure. It moved with every step, creating imbalance in my brain and my body. We need to widen our field of choices.

There are a hundred thousand species of love, separately invented, each more ingenious than the last, and every one of them keeps making things.

—Richard Powers
The Overstory

Relationships can be steadfast, loyal, and supportive. There are also those that are rocky, tentative, and uncommitted. These connective relationships may be within a family, within our work environment or in community. Many crisscross these domains. We continually create new relationships while others evolve or end. What many have not understood is that all our relationships affect each other although usually without our awareness. The constellations in the sky have configurations while also being a part of a larger galaxy, universe, and cosmos.

A3: Acknowledge, Accept, Allow

One formula that is useful for individuals, groups, and collections of people to bridge relationship or communication is what I named the A3 process: Acknowledge, Allow, Accept. The first step is to acknowledge what is true for self about facts, feelings and values. Step two is to acknowledge what is true for another, according to what is conveyed verbally and non-verbally. It is necessary to clear the mind, be present and listen to accept what is valid for self and other. Allowing in this process means to let every individual own their personal reality without judgment. When we are judging we are holding implicit bias about right or wrong, good or bad, true, or untrue. When I enter this process by myself or with others, I am required to let go of assumptions, open to something new, unseen or forgotten, and sit in a space, waiting for a new revelation to emerge. The key is to find the links of common likeness that create some form of bridge to understand each other at a deeper level. Maybe it is simply to acknowledge that I don't know how to enlarge

Blueprint for Shaping Your Future

my degree of compassion for another, or to understand specificity on a topic, or how to move up to a more conceptual understanding. Allowing that I don't know what I don't know is a delicious space to sit.

© Pavel Konovalov

    My clients were typically ones that were trained to delve into levels of specificity I could not grasp. Engineers, scientists, physicians, and chemists dwelled in the depths of knowledge. My task was to enter their reality and lead them to wider perspectives. It was reciprocal as I was going deep with them to see their maps of reality. They adapted to go wide and bridge beyond their trained mental disciplines and accept emotion into relationships. We frequently truth-busted old beliefs to allow wider perspectives.

When my husband died unexpectedly, I was in the middle of a nine-month contract with a group of scientists at a lab in the northeast. Upon hearing of my loss, they offered to postpone our training. I declined and resumed my time with them after a short break because I was in relationship with each scientist who was in the process of personal change. Now I was in the same boat! I needed to continue as I accepted their support. The first session was awkward when I returned. No one knew how to handle that fragile situation.

My re-entry began my giving them tips about what I needed and how they could offer support. My world was turned upside down. I told them that my emotions were tender. Something might trigger a memory that was fresh, and I undoubtedly would not be able to hide my emotion. "What I ask is that if you detect such a moment, please just hold space for me to recover." I explained I did not expect them to console me, but simply to BE with me in a quiet moment. The group breathed a sigh of relief with the understanding that emotion is real and though not part of their group relations, they were given unstated permission that they too could incorporate empathy into our communications. They began to understand that suppressing feelings leads to miscommunication. Transformation occurred as an unexpected consequence of my tragedy. A shaky bridge connected us human-to-human.

Blueprint for Shaping Your Future

The ability to take into consideration three points of view is essential to allow difference without blame and judgment. First person point of view describes what I see from my eyes, hear from my ears, and feel in my body which allows me to experience me. Second-person point of view can only partially replicate what another person sees, hears, feels by imagining through all discernable information given, verbal and non-verbal. Third point of view is neutral, like a camera. It only records what it sees and hears with no other interpretation.

The neutral viewpoint is the most difficult since it is not easy to let go of preconceived thoughts. Just the facts! Like bystanders who observe a car accident from three corners of an intersection, it can be a messy description of reality. After acknowledging all viewpoints, it is necessary to allow each one as valid. Accept that there may be similarities and differences without judgment of right or wrong, good or bad. We learn to hold a space for multiple realities.

There are several things to consider when we pick up a camera. The camera views life and objects from a neutral point of view. It simply records what it sees. Considering which lens and what speed to set the camera, it can focus on the details, zoom out to a landscape or wide angle. No sound is captured in still life photos. Choose color or black and white. Capture stillness or movement. The observer interprets the overlap of personal reality. Sometimes it is useful to reflectively observe life as a series of photographs as a way to hone the skill of observation.

When I look at family photographs for which I have no memory, I observe differently than if attached to an incidental memory. Where and when was the photo taken? What was the specific context? Looking at photos that evoke memories, I move into subjective mode, not the unbiased bystander.

Life can become unbalanced and out of focus. Becoming skilled as an observer adds room for new perspective. Looking in the rearview mirror of memories, I realized how much time as a concept has affected my perceptions. I gain insight when I take out the artificial equation we call time.

Time Collapses

In consciousness there is no separation between past, present, and future even if measured by 1500 miles of highway, according to Russell Targ, a laser physicist, and teams of scientists funded by the government. They proved that accuracy and reliability for remote viewing is not dependent on distance or time. Wikipedia defines remote viewing (RV) as the practice of seeing impressions about a distant or unseen target, purportedly "sensing" with the mind. In my world I often experience timeless awareness that is spacious. The concept of remote viewing helped me explain the women's voices I sensed in the castle outside of Edinburgh, Scotland. But when it happened, I was clueless to understand.

My first break-up with time, as an example, occurred as I was preparing to travel with a group of anthropologists to Peru. My Rolex watch quit working. Truly. I left it behind and eventually sold it. The clock by my bedside stopped, and my computer went haywire. In that situation I did not realize it was a foreshadowing of how I would recalibrate to the concept of time high in the Andes with the Q'ero communities. And so it began. I literally began to intuit past, present, and future meshed together without delineation. My Andean teachers showed me relationships between the planet and the stars that offered a broader scope of my limited understanding.

Fierce Love for Community

Recently I interviewed one of the Community Weavers in my town. She is a person known for her "fierce" love of our village. I asked how she described loving in such a way. "I feel it deeply in my gut," she explained. "It's like the love I have for my children. Keeping them safe, seeing them grow in healthy ways and giving them an environment so they can thrive." "Like a mama bear?" I asked. "More like a mother tiger!" she exclaimed.

Loving fiercely has a depth of passion that is undeniable. This love is active and continuous. If we think about what we are passionate about, the intensity of the emotion increases. Musicians and artists come to mind because the passion can be seen visually or with sound and is typically shared!

The most successful community model I've heard about is one introduced to me by another long-time local visionary. "Collective impact is the commitment of a group of actors from different sectors to a common agenda for solving social problems, using a structured form of collaboration" (Wikipedia). The Collective Impact Model harnesses the will of the people when there are networks that are aligned for purpose.

My question for each of us, is what do we love so much in our life or our community, or the planet, that we are willing to change something inside ourselves or commit to actions that show our fierce love?

A Community Story

Living in a small village has allowed me to be deeply rooted and intertwined across the breadth and depth of my community. Having gone through two significant floods, an extraordinary winter's freeze in which we lost electricity and water, and long periods of drought, has provided multiple opportunities to connect with those in crisis and those who were ever-present in supportive roles. We were in it for ALL of us. Bias and demarcations of difference faded away.

Where is it possible to participate on boards, councils, in town halls to deliberate as community? Sitting on the sidelines leaves out information, knowledge, and wisdom which are available when we gather collectively to find common objectives.

Blueprint for Shaping Your Future

When we try to pick out anything by itself, we find it hitched to everything else in the universe.

— John Muir
Conservationist

After 9/11, the world changed. After fifteen plus years working with companies in their organizational development, the timing for such work changed because of travel restrictions, softness in the global economy and needs to refocus. After completing the projects that were underway, I felt a call to take a pause.

When I moved back to Texas after my husband's death, I had chosen a small village in the hill country off the beaten path between Austin and San Antonio. My heart longed for community, but I had been traveling constantly. A call to put down new roots took me on another pathway. Who am I in this place and space?

Living amid nature surrounded by old oaks and juniper and not far from the Blanco River and Cypress Creek, I began to explore. Remnants of past civilizations are evident here. Undomesticated wildlife still exists, including mountain lions whose migration path along streams and rivers bless the natural environment. Curiously, I have had many experiences with these feline animal beings in dreams and real life.

Still needing to work, I had an epiphany one day as I was driving through our small town. On my right I noticed a building that had been unoccupied for some time. An image formed in my mind: That structure looks like a giant Tikki Hut! As the story unfolded, I found myself in a long-term lease with a vision for a community gathering place in the form of a coffee and smoothie shop.

Using the idea of a community gathering place as my vision, the idea manifested into a 1600 square foot reality including internal demolition, restoration and an architectural plan. The principles underlying the Hawaiian culture of 'aloha,' an inclusive greeting when meeting or departing with another person, and the underlying sense of Ohana as family resonated with me. Our motto became:

MANAWALE'A

Do all the good you can.
By all the means you can.
In all the ways you can.
In all the places you can.
At all the times you can.
To all the people you can.
As long as ever you can.

Blueprint for Shaping Your Future

—Anonymous

My joy grew as community gathered. Aging, young, professionals, laborers, educators, and health-minded people showed up again and again. Engagements, support groups, poetry readings, and open-mic monthly events knitted into relational weavings through floods, rainy seasons, drought and sunshine.

Our baristas, often college aged needing part-time work, were stars. They were beloved to me as I saw them mature during our tenure together. I trusted the process and it worked well.

It was a steep learning curve since I had no previous retail experience. Inventory, distribution, payroll and taxes for a brick-and-mortar were unknown to me. Because I was deeply committed to my vision, I found the stamina to forge ahead.

After twelve years and a busted kneecap, I began to see signals that called me to slow down and refocus again! It was excruciating to consider the thought of letting go of this heart space that had served so well to locals and visitors. Eventually, I decided to let go. Another deep surrender to trust that it was time for a change. Another version of the shop exists today. I am delighted to imbibe in someone else's vision and a different sense of community identity to be honored.

Knowing when to hold 'em and when to fold 'em as the song goes is not easy. It's not only a mental decision, but more about aligning with messages from the heart and trusting your deepest intuition. Unless the three triangulation points of head, heart and gut are aligned with a resonant "yes," the decision needs more cooking time.

This is the intersection where commitment comes into play. Are we willing to sit in the incubation period long enough to commit to what matters most, not what is expected from the outside world?

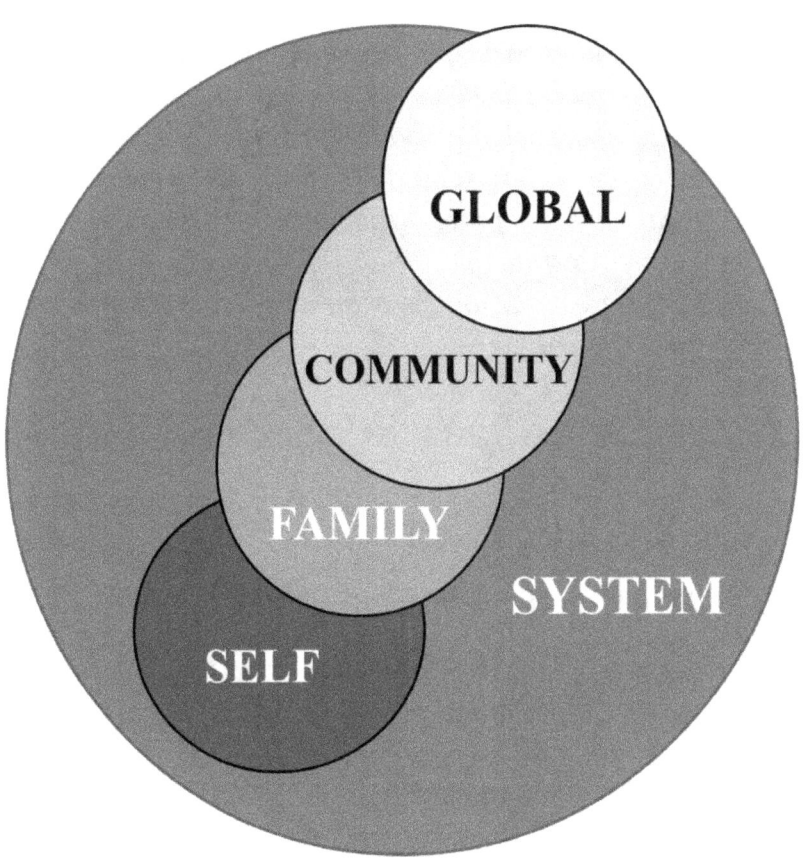

© DuAnne Redus

Blueprint for Shaping Your Future

Dimension VI: Ability to balance/rebalance internally as reflected by the cycles of nature

The law of physics says that a bee cannot fly. The aerodynamic principle says that the breadth of its wings is too small to keep its huge body in flight, but a bee doesn't know. The bee doesn't know anything about physics or its logic and flies anyway. This is what we can all do. We can fly and prevail in every moment in the face of any difficulty and in any circumstance despite what they say. Let us be bees, no matter the size of our wings. May we all take flight and enjoy the pollen of life.

—Author unknown,
NASA poster

Mother Nature

The shock waves of life come and go as we face catastrophes that show how humankind is beginning to face the consequences of interfering with the ecology of our earth system. Deforestation, extraction of natural resources, depleting surface water, air pollution and attempts to dominate the wilderness have brought us to a tipping point to acknowledge we have over-stepped and thwarted our relationship to our earth ship.

If we choose to take the observer role, we see vivid examples of elegance in the natural world. Animal migration is one pattern that is informative in relationship to change. Movement of groups, usually on a seasonal basis, is the most common form of migration. It is found in all major animal groups, including birds, mammals, fish, reptiles, amphibians, insects, and crustaceans. The trigger for the migration may be local climate, local availability of food, the season of the year or for mating. Intuitively, the timing and need is sensed to make changes. Instinctively they know consequences will follow if changes are not made.

Geese Flying in V-formation demonstrates shared leadership. When the leader of the V-form gets tired, it passes behind and another goose immediately takes over the lead. The geese that fly behind croak their support for the leader. If a goose gets sick or injured, two more geese come out of formation to follow and protect the injured one. Geese mourn when they lose a mate or eggs. They are loyal and mate for life with a partner. Geese have strong feelings of affection for the other members of the group.

Who hasn't felt the sense of awe when standing next to a thousand-year-old tree, or stood on the rim of the Grand Canyon, or viewed the night sky from a dark environment, or viewed fields of lavender blowing in the breeze?

One of my teachers describes these beautiful experiences as being connected to the Salka or wild undomesticated energy as I've mentioned before. He describes this energy as being in service of the domesticated, worldly energy which can become overly mechanized, systematic, and out of balance with the natural world. These energies are like two sides of the same coin.

© Stoupa

Two Sides of the Same Coin

Accountability and responsibility are similar. When individuals are responsible and accountable for their actions, they are more empowered. Organizations hold the same key to be responsible and accountable for agreements made and kept. Systems thinking is a breakthrough to elevate problem-solving, innovation, and re-engineering where timing and context matter. Unintended consequences can be readily seen and traced. If the starting point considers consequences for the short and long term, product designers, service designers, economic designers will see the connections that impact lives, localities, communities, states, and nations from a universal view. What are the criteria to design a healthy organization that adapts and re-organizes as needed?

Opportunities with Evolving Technology and Science

Perseverance, NASA's Rover, landed on Mars with the *Ingenuity* helicopter attached to its belly in the context of a pandemic and weather crises on planet Earth. The mission was called Mars 2020. Successful landing was accomplished on February 18, 2021, demonstrating how a focused, long-term mission is accomplished with the collective minds of individuals who were committed to a common goal to seek signs of ancient life and collect samples of rock and possible soil for eventual return to Earth. *Mastcam-Z*, an advanced camera system, relays photos never-before seen. How do we replicate projects that bring this kind of vision to our disconnected sense of who we are as collective humanity?

Science and technology continue to reveal possibilities once thought fantasy. But on the other side of the coin, current disruptions and dehumanizing events continue to reveal lack of commitment to the egalitarian principles in the U.S. Constitution. Truth about the history of a nation that used slavery as free labor in its earliest settlements continues to show many perspectives that have been obscured in the history books. We, as a collection of diverse humans are at the crux of re-imagining the continuing story to create the experiment of democracy that was once a dream. Our

Blueprint for Shaping Your Future

system of governance has tipped out of balance with disparities so wide and deep that it is in decay. The time has come for nurturance and sowing seeds for restoration. There is a clarion call for authentic leaders who are caring, creative, and critical thinkers to use imagination that delves into dimensions of infinite possibilities.

Micro-factories and zero-waste circular economies are one pathway to be considered. Recently I heard about how plastics are being repurposed into bricks in Nairobi, Africa. Nzambi Matee considered the great Pacific garbage patch that is continuously shipped away from the sources of waste to third-world countries. Matee, a materials engineer, built a machine to compress, then bake plastic hand-picked from landfills, forming building bricks that are 35% cheaper and up to seven times stronger than traditional bricks.

In Mumbai, India, plastic pollution was the impetus to use plastics to replace coal as fuel. Recycled tires are also used as fuel to produce green steel.

Veena Sahajwella, also known as the *Waste Queen* in Australia, Professor of Materials Science, and inventor of green steel, is also contributing to the "materials revolution." Born in India, she moved to Australia and has widely contributed to what is known as a circular economy which is a regenerative system which resources input and waste, emission, and energy leaking for production within a geographic region to combat climate change. The concept is to transform problematic waste into sustainable methods like micro-factories to deconstruct waste where it is produced instead of shipping it away from its source.

Fusion of Science and Technology
Quantum physics, cybernetics, natural science, kinesiology, nutritional science, and social science each have sets of principles from which they operate and evolve. Dissolving boundaries between the accepted practices offers new territory for exploration. The wide array presents opportunities for humans to make wide and rich choices in life and work. Competing with the most real or most accurate maps of reality seems less compelling than to see the connections among them all. The frontier of human development and how we decide to interact is indeed energy in motion.

Beyond Amateur Humans
At the highest level, the boardroom metaphor encompasses tables of all kinds scattered throughout communities where honest conversations acknowledge, allow, and accept the reality that systems need to evolve, repair, and restore the cellular structure of the mass system of humanity as we evolve from amateur humans. In this sense every human is needed as a leader who takes responsibility and accountability for the common good choosing how we pollinate the future. As we become accountable and responsible to each other and the planet, we are writing our legacy for future generations.

Blueprint for Shaping Your Future

The formula to continue to expand our sense of identity with our clear voice as we travel new and unknown pathways by increasing our ability and willingness to face conflict and paradox head on, will assist us to bridge relationships as we continually rebalance internally, just like the cycles of nature. We will collectively demonstrate our commitment to become *Sapien Sapiens* who are connected to our earth home. Emerging visions are arising beyond mission impossible to infinite possible missions.

DuAnne Redus

The Balancing Act

*That great sunball that sustains us
can kill us as well,
if we overdo.
Heat stroke, heat exhaustion, dehydration,
death by cancer and its thousand swords.
Too much, too many of us, too many times.*

*No sun? A lack of vitamin D, a loss -
bereft of our sustaining life force energy.
No garden veggies without photosynthesis
All alive would wither and die without it.
A balance: not too much, but just
enough*

*How can we learn to balance ourselves like the sun
does?
Saving some to rise anew each day, refreshed
and ready for our new daily beginning.
How can we expend all energy in the precious hope of
guaranteeing we will rise again?
How do we come to learn and know the true nature of
our being naturally, as the sun knows?*

*Not too much but just enough?
We spend our lifetime evolving,
seeking into this perfect balance
that is our innate ability.*

—Jane Vaniger

Blueprint for Shaping Your Future

Epilogue

The Indian Boy's Raft

Many years ago, before the western frontier was "tamed," a young Indian boy's initiation into manhood was to be sent on a mission to find a kindred tribe. As he traveled on his journey, he noticed he was being tracked by something unknown just as he came upon a vast stretch of water. A river he knew little about.

There were no boats or bridges to cross the wide water. With his sense of impending danger, he used his keen awareness to find the best resources for his immediate situation. He looked around to quickly identify the tall grass, sticks and nearby branches to build a sturdy raft. At the same time, he tuned in to his inner warrior who assured him he had all the skills he needed in this moment.

After riding the raft to a safe place on the opposite side of the river, the boy was no longer afraid and tuned in to his inner compass to feel grateful for his experience. Now he had another decision to make. Should he carry the raft with him into the unknown territory, or having gained the usefulness of the raft, leave it behind? After checking it out with his inner Guardian, he became certain it was best to leave the raft behind so he would be unburdened for the remainder of his quest.

The boy's Wisdom Guide comforted him with knowledge that he was on the right track to find kindred spirits. He was confident that he would continue to find resources along the way as they were needed. Someone or something would always be there to teach him what he needed to know or provide whatever he needed.

Along his path the boy-becoming-man had a vision that one day he would be given the knowledge to build a raft of the finest aged wood gathered from wherever he was at the time. He foresaw the craft would be more than adequate to carry himself through the remainder of his life journey, and that it would be large enough and strong enough to carry others who wanted to go along with him.

Blueprint for Shaping Your Future

Summarizing Essay
A Seer Sees from Behind the Eyes

We don't see the world as it is; we see the world as we are.

—Anais Nin

When I was fourteen, all I wanted was to get rid of my thick eyeglasses and wear contact lenses. I was so near-sighted I could barely see my hand in front of my face. I begged my parents for contact lenses, but with six children, my looks were not their highest priority. My grandmother encouraged me to accept my fate and be patient. "There is more to see than the outside," she said. "There's depth in everything. A Seer sees from the inside out."

Twenty-five years later, on my own and wearing contacts, the wisdom of Grandmother's message became clear in the Goblin Valley of southern Utah. "Please come with me to the renewal retreat," my close friend Sherry pleaded. "It'll be another great adventure with Shaman Americo. Tell me you'll go."

"Bad timing," I said reflecting on the kindred spirits we'd been with the previous year on a shamanic journey high into the Andes with Don Americo Yabar, a Peruvian mystic and poet. "I'd love to reconnect with the group who went to Peru with us, but I'm scheduled to negotiate a business contract in Boise, so, I'd need to leave the retreat early."

Sherry agreed we'd drive to the retreat, spend a few days and then we'd head to Boise. On the four-hour journey south from Salt Lake into the high desert wilderness, Sherry's funny stories filled our travel. Laugh lines swirled around her eyes, this joyous soul sister.

As we drove into the Wasatch Mountains leaving the densely populated valley behind, a wave of relief eased business worries in my mind. We descended from the high benches of the mountains into the desert of the San Rafael Swell where cacti spread over the terrain, sage fragranced the autumn air and red rock walls dominated. The changing topography hinted of the inner shift to come.

Sherry and I were the last of the thirty participants to arrive at the campsite near Goblin Valley State Park. A wilderness outfitter had erected large tents for sleeping, eating and meal preparation. Just after dark, we found the group circled around a large campfire. The blazing fire popped with the scent of cedar.

"Waiki! This feels like a homecoming." Americo greeted us, his dark eyes shining in the dim light. His subtle energy was magnetic. Small-boned, with latte colored skin, his black curly hair was tamed by his well-worn fedora. Don Americo spoke a combination of Spanish and Quechua, the native language of the Q'ero, the last descendants of the Inca. His foreign tongue enhanced my connection to his mystical teachings.

Blueprint for Shaping Your Future

"Sit," he gently urged, motioning with his hands as we joined the circle.

I took a deep breath. This did feel like a homecoming. My eyes scanned the circle. Directly across sat Big Bad John, a retired military officer who had spent his life fighting world battles. His large frame was layered with a traditional button-down collared-shirt and sweater, his demeanor serious. His arms were crossed tightly over his chest, as if protecting his heart. Close-cut, dark hair sprinkled with gray contrasted with his ruddy face. "Something inside me is afraid. Even after facing terrorists and living to tell about it, I have no peace." John was answering the why-are-you-here question.

Alister, a rugged young man, appeared comfortable in his wooly green sweater, hiking boots and jeans but his unshaven face looked stiff and frozen. "After our last journey when I returned home to Ireland, I knew that the Andes was only a beginning." He paused and stared into the fire. "The beginning of what, I'm not sure. But I'm ready to continue this journey into connection with Pachamama."

The group sighed at the mention of this sacred word. Pachamama is the Quechua term for mother earth. Our travels together had taken us into the Peruvian highlands. We had stayed with the indigenous Mollomarka people who live in balance with Pachamama.

Wind swirled the fire, blew white smoke over the tall rocks and up toward the rising moon, Mama Quilla.

Gwen, wrapped in a magenta shawl, spoke next. Her quiet shy voice matched her delicate features. "I want a cleansing. My energy is out of whack. I cry all the time and take everything personally. I feel disconnected from my spirit." Around the circle, folks nodded in agreement. Her round blue eyes spilled large drops as she looked at each friend.

In the Andes, the native people don't differentiate between good and bad. All energy is either sami, light, or the opposite hucha, heavy. Heavy energy feels unsettled, ill, or out of sorts. The group energy felt hucha, heavy. Maybe this wasn't going to be the vacation I had imagined.

"How often do you dismiss the inner knowing of your heart, and trust only your head?" Americo questioned us. I felt my spirit teacher's presence as strongly as if he'd reached across the fire and touched me. What am I going to say? Inside my conscious mind I intuitively knew it was time to move forward. Was I ready to delve deeper into inner guidance?

"Once we begin the inner journey home, Spirit continues to call us," Americo said. What if I lose it? Am I crazy? Americo's black eyes seared through my awareness. He focused beyond my fear. Then I knew. This retreat was the most important place in the world for me to be. This Utah retreat was the continuation of the spiritual journey we'd begun a year ago, high in the eastern Peruvian slopes. How could I have known that this group and Americo would work together for another six years?

Blueprint for Shaping Your Future

My voice quivered. "I'm learning to trust," I said. "This is an ongoing, collective experience. It's about more than me."

Americo continued. "The Q'ero were spiritual advisors to the Inca. They are weavers of a spiritual bridge of love, between cultures and beyond what humans experience as time. Are you willing to settle into your being and begin?"

"I'm willing to let go of my schedule," I said, knowing that Sherry was willing to go or stay. "I want to stay in this circle." Still, I trembled, and thoughts jabbed my consciousness. How will I pay my mortgage if I don't get this contract? Turning my back on business is irrational! What am I thinking? Fear gnarled my stomach, yet I recalled other spiritual pursuits where I'd let go of material things —a long-term corporate job, the control of my adult children, and I had lived well through the change. Be careful of your own suffering because it is easy to love it, Americo's words popped into my head. Secretly I yearned to understand the dynamics of control and surrender - the philosophical foundation of this Peruvian teacher.

As the campfire blazed, Americo danced on the rocks and spoke in his poetic, sing-song Spanish. "Everything is connected," he said. "The rocks to the trees to the stars. Humankind has forgotten that ALL is One and that the universe is perfectly orchestrated to a rhythm we no longer remember." Aha! My teacher is here to unteach me. "Remove the mind," he said. "It is only meant to serve the heart."

The mind is meant to serve the heart. That statement sent me into a tizzy. Layers of cultural beliefs and inbred push-to-achieve patterns started falling away, like dead leaves from a tree. The feeling of surrender was similar to the release I'd had when we'd been close to Apu, the mountain spirit of Peru.

During our ten days and nights in the Utah wilderness, physical nourishment was filled by the outfitter's scrumptious meals, while Americo fed our spirits. He delighted in surprises. He asked us to run like rabbits escaping a cougar. He told us to find a hiding place in the rocks that felt like our personal nest in nature. He planned an all-night trek of which we were unaware.

We carpooled to Goblin Valley State Park. Burnt orange sandstone formations with sheer cliffs and tall spires, carved by ancient winds and swift water, greeted us at the entry. We gathered around the Three Sisters rock formation.

"It's time to be silent," Americo announced. "When the sun disappears in the west, we will remain quiet from dusk-to-dawn." Wait a minute. What if I need help? What-ifs stormed through my mind, while fear stomped across my chest. My heart raced. Slow breathing mellowed me. Inhale and hold for a count of four, exhale and hold for a count of six. Inhale slowly, exhale slowly. Soon a quiet presence came over me and a new thought popped into my head. I want to know my Self in the context of the wild, and I want to enter its mystery. What did that mean? The evening air chilled me. I pulled my red alpaca poncho out of my sling bag.

Blueprint for Shaping Your Future

In Peru, we had been introduced to the Iloq'e world - non-ordinary, mysterious. The high-village peoples accept the Iloq'e, left side, like the hemispheres of our brain, as connected to the natural flow of life. But I felt stuck in pana, the right side or logical, schedule-driven world. It's one thing to learn shamanic techniques, another to connect to the ancient Incan teachings.

My eyes felt like sandpaper. The bone-dry air irritated my contacts. I decided to trust my inner knowing. I would follow my intuition, my insight, moment-by-moment, step-by-step, a blind person groping in the dark. I removed my contact lenses. Am I up to this? It's dangerous to go without seeing.

Severe myopia lived behind my green eyes. I had read *You Can Heal Your Life* by Louise Hays who suggested that myopia is related "to fear of the future" and "not trusting what is ahead." Those concepts fit. I wanted to exorcise my fear, as well as the resentment I harbored toward my father for endowing me with his bad eyesight. A cold sweat poured through my skin. I recalled one of Americo's directives, "Connect to light threads." Filaments of light are like an aura, but different. Americo had taught that all living things have filaments - delicate, purposeful threads of light as clearly seen as a spider web. "When the heart opens, we see things unseen," he had said. "Filaments hold everything in love. Where there is love there can be no fear."

Where there is love there can be no fear. I breathe in love; I breathe out fear. Over and over, I repeated this mantra.

As the sun dropped in the western sky, our group faced the Three Sisters formation--simple feminine forms with veiled faces. Eight to ten feet tall, the three stone shapes, stair-stepped in height. I'm one of three sisters. I felt connected to the orange-red rocks now bathed in the light of the setting sun. A rainbow bathed the sandstone sisters and a blessing flowed from my heart. Accept this moment with joy. I relaxed. The adventure had begun.

Don Americo led the group into the ghoulish valley. Carrying only walking sticks, small knapsacks, and water, we stepped quickly behind him, a gaggle of geese following our mother. He ambled with the grace of a deer, his shoulder length hair brushing the top of his hand-woven tunic. I wanted to attach myself to him like a shadow so I would not get lost. Trusting someone else again, instead of myself? The last ebb of sunlight faded. Darkness enveloped us and my awareness turned inward. After a while, the group's rhythm shifted from follow-the-leader to a collective human entity winding into the wilderness. Like an aboriginal walkabout, time and space disappeared. We became a living organism snaking through the boulders.

Goblin Valley State Park is only a mile across and two miles long. Yet, into the night, we zigzagged miles away from the Three Sisters. The air was cold, and the desert filled with ghostly silence, yet alive with sounds I could not name. Was the yapping, coyotes? Was the screeching an owl? The moon shone eerily on the boulders and pinnacles that resembled animals, trolls, and gremlins bigger than life. Were they watching me?

Blueprint for Shaping Your Future

We stopped to rest and to deepen into our experience. But as soon as I reached a meditative state, Americo took off in another direction. My senses became more acute. The wind cooed. I felt it from several directions. Mama Tuta, the gift of night, reminded me of Peru. Aromas surrounded me - dirt, sage, life. In the surreal silence I wandered slowly and carefully, unable to see where my feet would land. Connect with the filaments. Connect with love. I raised my left hand and then my right hand toward the night canopy and imagined I was connecting to the subtle energy webs, moonbeams.

In previous sessions, Americo had taught us to lie on the ground and observe the breath of nature, to place our bellies against large boulders, and become sensitive to our presence in the natural world. He taught us to communicate with trees, placing our palms on the trunk, asking the tree for its story and to walk without looking at our feet. "In this darkness," he had said, "more of the natural world will reveal itself. The stars, *estrellia*, are energetic beings to guide you."

I sensed salka, the term for wild, undomesticated energy, especially present in the natural world untamed by humans. The Inca ancestors believed salka to be a vital connection to the universe. This pure energy is like the essence of a child's innocent laughter or the feeling that comes from looking deeply into the eyes of an animal who trusts you. Through the top of my head salka, raw, wild energy, entered my body.

Hours into our sojourn we entered a space where the path underfoot changed. Through my soft-soled moccasins the dirt felt firm instead of loose and sandy.

Above me, rock walls towered. Even with my blurry vision, silhouettes outlined symmetrical spires of a sandstone cathedral. My heart pounded in reverence; being in this sacred space was more awe-inspiring than any church or temple I'd ever entered. Like a gargantuan tuning fork, the rocks magnified our vibrations with palpable energy. In slow motion, like a Tai Chi exercise, we scooped up energy balls, shaped them and tossed them to one another like bean bags. The group sighed and circled under the blanket of stars, for my eyes, pinpricks of whiteness. As the subtle light played on the stones, a sense of inner peace filled my heart. Homecoming.

    Americo's mellow voice broke the silence. "Walk outward and find a spot to be alone. You will know when it is time to return."

    But I was comfortable here. The idea of pushing further into the night, alone, disturbed me. I breathed deeply; followed instructions, letting my intuitive insight lead the way. Drawn to an enclosed niche with a gnarled juniper at the entrance, I reached down and placed my hands on a large stone. Instantly, I recognized the shape of a puma. For years, the puma, a sacred animal in the Inca tradition, had been central to my dream world. The puma, cousin to the jaguar, cougar, and mountain lion, is a secretive, solitary, nocturnal creature. I remembered a recent dream where I was at the bottom of a deep chasm. At the top, on one side, was an enormous yellow puma staring at me, transmitting its innate strength and power. On the opposite side of the crevasse was a tall barbed-wire

Blueprint for Shaping Your Future

fence and behind that, a prison. A guard there, with a rifle, had me in his sight. Then in the dream, my sight was suddenly clear. Would my sight or my insight become clear now?

In the dream, as well as in the moment, I reached for the puma. The stone body of the rock animal radiated heat, stored from the day's sun. It provided me with a warm blanket of comfort. I sat down, relaxed, feeling safe, and then slipped into a meditative trance, dreaming and journeying. Toward morning I had a vision of my dad's face in a puma body. "Accept what is yours," he said. "See value in every part of your body." I had blamed Dad and others, and in so doing had set myself up to feel lost and alone. It was time to let go. My heart opened like a clam in spring water. The rush felt like a source of energy I can only call Truth - both sharp and comforting. I felt light enough to fly. My eyes saw distinct shapes in the rocks and tree branches around me that moments ago, were invisible. No longer am I separate. I am connected to Salka, energy wild and free.

At dawn's first light, I kissed the ground and said goodbye to my stone puma. Clicking sounds called me back. Sherry and other friends were playing a simple two-beat rhythm with hand-held stones. Spontaneously, all of us formed a circle and danced. Our spiral movements were so graceful and harmonious, it seemed we had danced together forever. Above, the moon and sun began their exchange waltz and the ancient stone spirits nearby joined us, as all shuffled joyfully with Pachamama. It was a new sense of communion— a loving bond to the rocks, the group, the earth, and me. Homecoming!

As sunlight stretched over the eastern horizon, we wound our way back toward the Three Sisters, connected and disconnected, inward and outward, alone and one. Finally, I felt at peace with my duality— both the spiritual and mundane. I recalled how the Hopi people refer to the Soul's journey: the old, fallen-down Self, the Self living in the now and the Self under construction. I recognized all three. Past, present and future within myself. I saw myself as a filament in the pattern of the Divine Matrix, a thread in the web of the universe.

As I left Goblin Valley, the Three Sisters sent me a message. I recognized Grandmother's words, "A Seer sees from the inside out." The Seer seeing beyond space and time was me allowing my intuitive insight.

Blueprint for Shaping Your Future

References

Andreas, Connirae, *Core Transformation*
Barlow, Ph.D. Marjorie R., *The Possible Woman*
Barks, Coleman, *The Essential Rumi*
Braden, Gregg, *The Divine Matrix*
Campbell, Joseph, *The Power of Myth*
Diltz, Robert, *Tools for Dreamers*
Eisler, Riane, *The Chalice & The Blade*
Eisler, Riane and Fry, Douglas P., *Nurturing Our Humanity*
Grosbois de, Teresa, *Mass Influence*
Hawking, Stephen, *Black Holes and Baby Universes*
Houston, Ph.D., Jean, *A Mythic Life*
Kelton, Stephanie, *The Deficit Myth*
Klotz-Douglas, Neil, *Desert Wisdom*
Lewin, Roger, *Complexity*
McGregor, Karen, *The Tao of Influence*
Mindell, Arnold, *Sitting in the Fire*
Myss, Caroline, *Sacred Contracts*
Russell, Peter, *The Global Brain Awakens*
Senge, Peter M. *The Fifth Discipline*
Toth, Angelyn, *Radical Trust*
Wheatley, Margaret J., *Leadership and the New Science*
Wheatley, Margaret J., *Who Do We Choose to Be?*
Whyte, David, *The Heart Aroused*
N.E. Thing Enterprises, *Magic Eye*

https://confidentleaderblueprint.blog

DuAnne Redus | LinkedIn

duanneredus - YouTube

https://www.amazon.com/author/duanneredus

https://soundcloud.com/duanneredus

ShaMama in the Boardroom (substack.com)

www.sixdimensionblueprint.com

www.ingramcontent.com/pod-product-compliance
Lightning Source LLC
Chambersburg PA
CBHW071512220526
45472CB00003B/992